Jesus Is Speaking to and
Through All Kinds of People

Jon and Pam Strain

You Gotta Listen
Jesus Is Speaking to and Through All Kinds of People
By You Gotta Ask, Inc. © 2023

The publisher of this book supports copyright. Copyright fuels creativity, encourages diverse voices, promotes free speech, and creates a vibrant culture. Thank you for buying an authorized edition of this book and for complying with copyright laws by not reproducing, scanning, or distributing any part of it in any form without permission. You are supporting writers and allowing authors to continue to publish books.

While the publisher and authors have used their best efforts in preparing this book, they make no representations or warranties with respect to the accuracy or completeness of this book and specifically disclaim any implied warranties or merchantability or fitness for a particular purpose. No warranty may be created or extended by sales representatives or written sales materials. The advice and strategies contained herein may not be suitable for your situation. You should consult with a professional where appropriate. The stories and interviews in this book are true although the names and identifiable information may have been changed to maintain confidentiality.

The publisher and authors shall have neither liability nor responsibility to any person or entity with respect to loss, damage, or injury caused or alleged to be caused directly or indirectly by the information contained in this book. The information presented herein is in no way intended as a substitute for counseling or other professional guidance.

All Bible references, except where otherwise noted, are from New American Standard Bible (NASB) translation. Used by permission. All rights reserved. www.lockman.org

Cover Concept and Logo Design: Tyler Penner Design
Lead Editor: Heather Goetter
Book Production: Aloha Publishing

Softcover ISBN: 978-1-7365901-3-3

Published by: You Gotta Ask, Inc.

Printed in the United States of America

DEDICATIN

We dedicate this book to our praying parents.

Norma Hill (Jon's mother) for her tenacity, daily lifting all her children and their spouses before the throne of grace. Her prayers moved the hound of heaven to put Jon up a tree—a spiritual evergreen. There would be no You Gotta Ask Ministry if she didn't ask, again and again.

Bob and Nadeen Boettger (Pam's parents) who, since they discovered the resources of Jesus Christ, did not cease to pray each morning together for all their daughters and their daughter's spouses, and then their grandchildren and their grandchildren's spouses. Because of their faithfulness and God's grace, every one of Bob and Nadeen's children and spouses as well as grandchildren and their spouses has a relationship with Jesus Christ.

How comfortable are you
with the idea that God wants to
communicate through you?

CONTENTS

Introduction	9
1: My Sheep Hear My Voice	19
2: The Most Important Thing	31
3: Laid Bare	41
4: You Can Trust That God Is Speaking	53
5: The Consequences of Obeying	63
6: If Jesus Did It . . .	75
7: God Is Bigger Than Injustice	83
8: The Three Barriers to Communicating With Christ	93
9: In the Still, Small Voice	109
10: Our True Identity	119
11: God's Words Can Deliver Us	131
12: Preparing for the Moment	139
13: Jesus, the Healer and Liberator	149
14: Our Identity From Conception	161
15: Hearing His Voice for Us and Our Children	173
16: God's Voice Is a Blessing	181
17: Names Mean Something	193
18: Plan Together	205
19: How God Speaks	213
20: It's Your Turn	227
Acknowledgments	231
About the Author	233
Appendix	235

INTRODUCTION

"If you gotta ask, you gotta be prepared to listen!" The essence of this book can be captured in this simple statement. It's a concept that follows naturally from our previous work, *You Gotta Ask*, where we explored how asking questions is a means of engaging in deep, genuine listening. By doing so, you learn, respond better to others, and make them feel respected and loved, fostering openness and a willingness to hear from us.

We want to introduce a unique element to the conversation: an incredibly influential third party—someone who knows both participants and can foster understanding. This third party is the triune God—Father, Son, and Spirit. Although unseen, God speaks to us softly, on a different frequency, as if through an earpiece.

But what if your conversation partner is unfamiliar with this third voice? While you may be learning to recognize God's voice and represent it, the other party might struggle to discern or accept it. God has asked us to listen and hear his voice so we can speak his words in a way the other party is accustomed to hearing. How comfortable are you with the idea that God wants to communicate through you?

This communication should be natural because it's part of our intrinsic design, yet many of us are not utilizing this potential. This leads us to the two main obstacles we'll explore in the book: First is our failure to recognize that God is speaking to us in a discernable way. Second, we may not be really listening to people, especially in a way that helps them discern that God might be communicating with them. God is speaking to and through all kinds of people and has been throughout their lives. Most people discern this in retrospect.

To illustrate how this three-party listening works, consider the following story.

SOCIAL INTERACTION: MORE THAN SMALL TALK

People often gauge the "social temperature" of others through initial impressions and small talk. However, this seemingly trivial interaction carries great significance.

Pete set his things on the table next to mine. He noticed that I was wearing a suit and tie, reading intently with my laptop open, and looking at a Bible commentary. When he asked about it, I mentioned I was preparing to lead a Bible study at the capitol. He made a very snide comment about God being the source of evil in the world. It didn't make any sense to me, except that it was a swipe at God, completely out of the wild blue yonder. I sensed a strong signal from the unseen conversation partner (God) not to react, comment, or challenge anything Pete said. I was just to *listen*.

> "Being a witness is helping them hear the voice of love that has always been speaking to them."
> — Jamie Winship

Though not how I want to start conversations in general, he dove into politics and political affiliation after exchanging names. He was a self-described "left of center-winger." This was no surprise because of where this Starbucks was located. His assumption about me was that I was a "right-winger" because I was preparing a Bible study for a heavily right-leaning state legislature. I offered him nothing about my views specifically because there was no indication he wanted to know.

After he purchased his coffee, he sat down next to me. Though not drawn to his personality, I decided to be intentional in conversation and ask only a question here and there—mostly listening. To get him started, I asked him a couple of questions about the news, weather, and sports, and then the listening began.

Eventually, I learned he was a retired park ranger, single, and 60-plus years old. I asked him about his career and learned he was job hunting and had been unsuccessful for quite a while. He began to tell me about his history with women (never married), his world travels (thus, no retirement money put away), and his consequent anxiety about being alone with no financial nest egg. I marveled at how much personal communication he was sharing.

This deluge of private information continued to flow freely for the next 30 minutes, leaving no doubt about his worldview, history, and life status. Up to this moment, I had shared nothing about myself. He never asked. Had he been questioned by a police officer about our encounter, he would have had nothing to share except my name and that I lead a Bible study at the capitol. Beyond this, he could have only shared about how he experienced me.

I think he was taking my "social temperature," and perhaps he was curious that I didn't take his opening snide comment about God as a personal offense. As he let personal information out, I gave him my full, nonjudgmental attention. He noticed. Then he made a seemingly non-sequitur observation:

"You are obviously pretty smart. You listen. That's more than I can say for most in your camp."

Hmmm. Insight bomb. He had clearly run into others "in my camp" and those encounters had created an emotional barrier to God for him. Honestly, I suspected I could have launched a serious debate on at least 27 points he made in our first 27 minutes. However, I had earned his trust by absorbing every one of his opinions without ideological retaliation. Now he was letting me know I had passed the "Pete relational bar exam."

With that new social capital in hand, I wasn't about to reveal the truth of the matter. Nor would I reveal that I disagreed with just about every viewpoint that came out of his mouth. But with mutual respect established, I decided to spend my social capital circling back about his opening comment about God.

I said, "Pete, about your comment earlier—do you really believe God is evil or responsible for evil?"

He looked at me for a moment, then replied, "No. I don't."

Hmmm . . .

Apparently, he had exaggerated the claim to test me. Maybe he hoped to filter out another Bible jerk. It seemed small talk was not small that day. Thankfully, the whispering voice of God in my mind's ear telling me to check myself and listen actively to all Pete had to say was not small either.

How did God know something would shift in Pete during that 30-minute warm-up conversation? God knows Pete. God knew that Pete needed a nonreactive listening ear that day. I pray that Pete continues to encounter more quietly listening God-followers.

HOW DO YOU KNOW IT'S GOD'S VOICE?

You gotta ask, "Jon, how did you know you heard God telling you to zip your lips in this conversation with Pete?" This is the life-changing question we will answer throughout this book.

There are 10 characteristics we will use to help discern if you're hearing God speaking or something else: speaking in your own head, hearing the voice of the evil one, or some other source.

The 10 S's will act as our guide to recognizing God's voice, functioning as a framework to understand His communication. They are observable, affirming characteristics found in many encounters with God as depicted in biblical stories and personal experiences. These include the "still, small voice" that Elijah heard (1 Kings 19:12b KJV) and the way Paul describes "combining spiritual thoughts with spiritual words" in 1 Corinthians 2:13b.

The 10 attributes are not a rigid formula; rather, they provide insight into how people connect with God's voice over time. This understanding will help you shift away from a reluctance to engage with hearing God's voice (default agnosticism) and allow yourself the opportunity to hear God, giving Him the benefit of the doubt.

It's likely God speaking when it is . . .

☑ 1. Scriptural

☑ 2. Smarter than you

☑ 3. Surprising ("What?!")

- ☑ 4. Specific (answer to an ask)
- ☑ 5. Succinct (one-liner)
- ☑ 6. Spot-on (customized)
- ☑ 7. Spiritually fruitful
- ☑ 8. Supported by spiritually gifted people
- ☑ 9. Salvation-minded
- ☑ 10. Serving others' best interests

> **"He is there and He is not silent."**
> **— Francis Schaeffer**

In an episode of *The Chosen*, Jesus engages in a conversation with one of his 12 apostles, James, the son of Alpheus, not to be confused with James, the brother of John and son of Zebedee. Known as "little James," he is a lesser-known figure and is portrayed as having a physical impairment that causes him to walk slowly. He starts by apologizing to Jesus because he is inarticulate and apprehensive about his communication ability. Jesus replies, "Slow to speak—that is a very good quality."

James goes on to share his concern about how he can administer healing to others in Jesus's name when he himself has not been healed. He is not as strong as the other apostles with whom he has just been commissioned to go out to other cities to minister healing, casting out demons and proclaiming, "The Kingdom of heaven is near."

Like many of us, he feels like an imposter who just doesn't measure up to the high calling of Jesus. Like James, we may say to ourselves, "I'm not strong enough, smart enough, articulate enough, or healed enough. I'm simply not enough." To this, Jesus says, "Enough, already!"

Jesus responds to James's concern with a surprising yet profound answer: "When you discover yourself finding true strength because of your weakness, and when you do great things in my name, in spite of this, the impact will last for generations . . . Little James, isn't it beautiful that you are giving to others without having received yourself? But have no doubt, you will be healed."

This conversation highlights the power of listening and the value of empathy that moves us toward ministry to others despite our weaknesses and shortcomings, knowing our own full healing will come in time. We are weak so we will find our strength in God to do His mission. We are strongest when we listen to God and act on His leading. Is there anything more important?

Since listening is essential to hearing God's heart for people and being able to communicate His heart to them, the upcoming chapters will guide you through the 10 S's as they appear throughout both the Old and New Testaments of the Bible, as well as in personal stories. As you progress from one chapter to the next, you'll be taught to recognize these characteristics, and you'll be inspired to attune yourself to His voice. Embracing this understanding promises a thrilling adventure.

"... The sheep hear his voice, and he calls his own sheep by name and leads them out. When he puts forth all his own, he goes ahead of them, and the sheep follow him because they know his voice." John 10:3b-4 NASB

"I lay down My life for the sheep. I have other sheep . . ." John 10:15b-16a NASB

"I must bring them also, and they will hear My voice . . ." John 10:16b NASB

MY SHEEP HEAR MY VOICE

My father was a cattle rancher, and my grandfather once managed a modest dairy farm. We kept a handful of milk cows for our personal use, and I would sometimes be tasked with milking them. To summon them for milking, we'd call out, "Come, boss." I was always puzzled by the phrase and wondered why the seemingly simple-minded cows would respond to it. Later, I discovered that "boss" derives from the Latin word *bos*, which translates to "cow." I was taken aback, thinking, "Do milk cows understand Latin?"

If sheep and cattle can be called by our voices, why can't humans hear the voice of God? We are hardwired (created by God) and software-installed (re-created through the Holy Spirit when saved) to hear God's voice.

BEING SHEEP

"My sheep hear my voice . . ." (John 10:27a KJV) In order to walk in a healthy relationship with God, we must accept that this statement from Jesus is true.

The Greek verb for "hear" in this verse is in the indicative mood, signifying a factual statement. Furthermore, it's in the present tense, meaning the action is continuous.

This isn't the first instance of Jesus using the term "hear" in John 10. Initially, He uses it when Jesus introduces the metaphor of the sheep: ". . . the sheep hear his voice, and he calls his own sheep by name and leads them out. When he has brought out all his own, he goes before them, and the sheep follow him, for they know his voice." (John 10:3b-4 NKJV)

Sheep are attuned to the voice of their shepherd. This is particularly true for shepherds in the Middle East. They assign unique names to each sheep. When the shepherd arrives to collect them after their night in the pen, he might whistle or use a specific call that the sheep identify. They know it's time to move, feed, and hydrate. Since they recognize his voice, he guides them from the front, and they willingly trail behind.

The second instance is in 10:16: "I have other sheep which are not of this fold. I must bring them also, and they will hear my voice [indicative future; a statement of fact] . . ."

Ask yourself this: Am I more driven and coerced or led by His voice? Do I even hear His voice?

Being led by His voice feels more personal and connected than the pushy methods of shepherding I've noticed in the Western world, particularly in the United States. Let's consider two examples that starkly differ from what Jesus portrays.

EASTERN VS. WESTERN SHEPHERDS

While trekking in the Boise foothills, I was unexpectedly met by a flock of sheep cresting the hill. Taken aback, I pondered whether it would be possible to **walk** amidst them. However, my attention quickly shifted to **the** formidable dog that was steering them. The canine look**ed as** though it might consider me a light snack. There was **no chance** I was venturing into the heart of its territory. Eventually, from the back, the shepherd made his presence known. I shouted, "Are we okay?" I was essentially asking, "Do **you have** this fierce dog under control?" He assured me, but I **was** still cautious to treat the dog with the utmost respect.

Every summer, we do a few **days of** hiking with our friends, Kelby and Connie Brown, in **Idaho's** Sawtooth Mountains. Loading the car early one **morning,** I was surprised again by a herd of sheep, coming down **the** street of Ketchum guided by smaller dogs and shepherds leading from the rear, whistling and shaking a can. This **biannual** event for decades has gotten sheep to and from summer pasture. Hustling to make our whitewater rafting appointment, I realized that there would be no driving through **the** parade of several hundred sheep clogging the street.

Both Eastern and Western shepherds achieve the task of guiding their sheep from one place **to** another. However, shepherds leading from the front using their voice offer a more serene approach compared to those driving from behind with the aid of dogs, whistles, **and** rattling cans. Throughout my brief interactions with the Western shepherds, I never once heard such a voice.

The fact that *we* can recognize the Shepherd's voice and that *I* have a unique name given by my Shepherd conveys a sense of intimacy and a close relationship with Him.

SAMUEL

Can we be taught like young Samuel to recognize God's voice?

"Now the boy Samuel was ministering to the LORD before Eli. And word from the LORD was rare in those days, visions were infrequent." (1 Sam 3:1)

"Now Samuel did not yet know the LORD, nor had the word of the LORD yet been revealed to him." (3:7) Eli prepared Samuel to recognize and respond to the voice of God, ". . . it shall be if He calls you, that you shall say, 'Speak, LORD, for Your servant is listening.'" (3:9) Samuel heard the voice (again) and when he responded and listened to the message, it turned out to be for Eli who had not been listening to God. Ironically, God called Eli to account through the boy he just trained to hear the voice of God! (3:10-18)

This story teaches us the following:

1. Hearing God's voice can be learned, if we know how to listen for it. (Samuel)

2. God's voice can be ignored, even if we know how to listen to it. (Eli)

3. God speaks to and through all kinds of people, surprisingly and spot-on. (A young boy)

4. The word of the Lord to us should not be rare. Are we listening after inviting Him to speak?

God has patiently increased my capacity to hear His voice over the years. I've always heard Him through Scripture, but now I am learning to hear Him directly and in many other ways.

AN UNEXPECTED ANSWER

For 18 months, our ministry had been praying fervently for an aggressive, high-risk outreach.

Former NFL Super Bowl-winning coach and NASCAR team owner Joe Gibbs addressed an audience of roughly 1,050 individuals, predominantly men, at the Caven-Williams Sports Complex at Boise State University. Round tables were filled with guests who were invited by 150 table hosts. The intention was to reach out to those whom our hosts believed needed to hear the message of Jesus Christ in their lives. Bryan Harsin, the BSU Football coach, graciously introduced Coach Gibbs. Gibbs not only delivered a spiritually enriching message but also presented each guest with a copy of his book, *Game Plan for Life*. Significant effort went into preparing our table hosts to select the right guests and engage them in meaningful, relationship-driven dialogue.

An unexpected glitch in the follow-up plan limited our capacity to connect with our guests, the main objective of the gathering. This situation caused a great deal of stress for me. I thought, "Lord, how can we navigate this? The intent behind the event is clear, but the way forward is muddled. There are numerous directions we could consider, yet none feel completely right. What is the best approach?" The dilemma kept me awake at night.

A few days later, standing in Starbucks, I encountered Coach Harsin, which was quite unusual, and we had a brief visit about the event. The very next day, at the same exact spot, my friend Robin walked in, whom I'd not seen for a long time. She had driven all night from out of state to watch her son's soccer game and needed coffee.

After catching up for a few minutes, she finally paused and said, "Jon, I have a picture coming into my mind, and I think it's for you from God, but I don't know what it means. May I share it with you?"

"Ahhh, okay." This was very unusual.

"In the picture, you are on a wide trail that comes to an abrupt end. There are several small trails to choose from. You are standing there unsure which to choose. The Father is saying, 'Choose any one of them because I will be with you; I trust you.'"

I was stunned and unable to speak. She had no way of knowing anything about the Gibbs event and my sleepless anxiety about event follow-up. I knew immediately what it meant and which trail I should take.

Recently, I saw Robin and shared the significance of that God-timed picture several years ago. She did not remember the occasion. She didn't know what it meant to me until now. She was simply obedient to what she heard. But how did I know it was God?

ASK. THIS. NOW.

Three Tools for Learning to Hear God's Voice Using the 10-S Indicators

1. Personal Reflection and Group Discussion

Personal reflection and group discussion points and questions follow each chapter. Jesus often used the phrase, "He who has ears to hear, let Him hear." (Matthew 13:9-23, 43) The Greek verb *akouo* (to hear) is in the imperative form (Matthew 13:9, 47) implying a command or strong admonition. "Hear and understand!" (Matthew 15:10) is another way to read it. Since Jesus delivered it in a group setting, it's better for us to explore truth in a group as well.

One tool to help you engage with every chapter is the 10-S indicators of God's voice found in the Appendix, which I invite you to flip to and ask yourself or your group these three questions:

a. Which of the 10 S's surprises you the most?

b. At a quick glance, is it plausible to you that most or even all 10 could be found in most stories, both Bible and personal, where God speaks to an individual?

c. Could this be a game-changer, quelling your uncertainty about hearing God?

2. Learning to Hear God's Voice: Identifying the 10-S Indicators

In the Appendix 10-S answer key (pages 235–254), 10-S indicators are identified for each Bible and personal story featured in chapters 1-19. The reader (or discussion group) can refer to it anytime while reading and personally reflecting or exploring in a group discussion. Reading and identifying the 10-S indicators in the Bible stories and personal stories in the Appendix will help you see new things in hearing God. We include Bible text with the indicators to accommodate personal and group discussion.

The Appendix content may be too much for some readers but necessary for others. Everyone should read through some to see that the 10 S's are legitimate indicators. However, some readers are built like me and want to see and judge for themselves, scrutinizing the details. The Appendix functions like an answer key. The reader may benefit from learning the 10 S's in the stories, then double-checking my claims by looking at the Appendix answers.

Why is this important? While we are created for communion with God, some things are not easy or intuitive.

3. Give God a Minute: Bullet-Point Journal

When I started planking (holding oneself in a push-up position), it was brutal. It seemed like on my first attempt I could only hold the position for a little bit.

With practice, a strong core developed and now I can hold a plank for quite a long time. Listening is like planking because it requires focused attention and practice. Listening well to anyone, even those we love most, can be difficult.

A "minute" of listening to God can be any length of time you want it to be. Why not start where you are? Something is better than nothing and chapter by chapter, day by day, your listening skills will develop. I have included a simple journal format I developed and use routinely.

Why is this important? I'm amazed at how many things I forgot that I asked and therefore miss the fact God answered! I'd simply moved on. It is very encouraging to me to recognize God is speaking and answering. Listening and watching through journaling has been a huge help. And I find that simple is best. I make sure to write down the big things, particularly the big three: pain, pressure, and purpose points. Since these are usually infested with fear, why not bring them to the God who is near? And documenting His responses builds faith and trust.

Each page is organized into two simple columns: Ask and Answer. As you will see on the accompanying page, I date the entries for reference because I plan to go back and review what I asked God to see if there was an answer. This makes me an attentive listener. Try it. You have a prompt at the end of each chapter.

Perhaps you will like the practice after reading this book and do as I do. I simply purchase an empty, wide-ruled composition book and fill in the basic format you will see on the next page.

JON & PAM STRAIN

GIVE GOD A MINUTE JOURNAL

	You Gotta *Ask*	You Gotta Listen & Watch *Answer*
Date: 11/06/23	PPP: What are my Pain and Pressure points? What Purposes should I pray about? **Scripture:** 1 Samuel 3:1-18—Hearing God's voice Can be learned; listen for it. (Samuel) • Can be ignored—with consequences. (Eli) • God speaks to and through all kinds of people—surprisingly & spot-on. (Young boy) • Shouldn't be rare. (3:1) • God, what else do I need to know about hearing your voice? What do I need to do? **PPP** • Mtg with K.G. today to resolve conflict. What is going on here that I don't see? • For my new Monday Bible study to come together (fear): chemistry, content • I'm feeling a lot of anxiety about the family holiday coming up. Why? Search my heart	11/09/23 Amazingly, all three of these 11/6 requests are about me trying to control things! Why do I have this need? What do I need to know?

THE MOST IMPORTANT THING

The disciples of Jesus comprised a variety of backgrounds and educations. However, during their three years together, they all overlooked the multiple instances where Jesus foretold His impending suffering, death, and resurrection. (Luke 9:22; Matt 16:21) It's perplexing how they missed His declaration as "the resurrection and the life" even as He raised people from the dead. (John 11; Luke 8:49-56) Equally puzzling is how the explicit angelic message to the women at the empty tomb was missed: "Why do you seek the living One among the dead? He is not here, but He has risen. Remember how He spoke to you while He was still in Galilee, saying that the Son of Man must be delivered into the hands of sinful men, and be crucified and on the third day rise again." (Luke 24:5b-7)

How do you miss the most important thing about the most important person in the room? The aware reader of Luke 24 should be nothing less than mentally screaming, "C'mon guys! Really?" How were they so slow to perceive the not-so-subtle messages that Jesus, the Christ, is risen from the dead? That very message is the Gospel—the greatest game-changing event in history.

The disciples missed the most important thing about the most important person on the scene when the women reported the heavenly messengers' message at the empty tomb of Jesus. "But these words appeared to them as nonsense, and they would not believe them." (Luke 24:11)

THE GOSPEL MESSAGE

The overwhelming and simple message of Scripture is that the God of the universe wants a relationship with each of us. He wants it so much that He came to Earth as a helpless baby, grew up among pain and diseases, and submitted Himself to His enemies to be tortured and die on the cross so He could have an eternal relationship with us.

If this is true, then why am I so slow to hear and perceive God's voice and presence as a way of life? The short answer is that it's a human thing, the fault of the great separation when sin came into the world, along with death, in Genesis 3. And I know that I am not alone in my aloneness. Like Samuel, we all need to learn to hear His voice—in Scripture and on the go.

Luke 24 gives us insight into how Jesus disrupts our slowness. In my head, I can still hear Dr. Wilbert Norton, former Dean of Wheaton Graduate School, quoting Jesus, who jolted the two men walking with Him on the road to Emmaus, "Oh foolish men [Dr. Norton translated it, "Fools!"] and slow of heart to believe in all that the prophets have spoken. Was it not necessary for the Christ to suffer these things and to enter into His glory?" (Luke 24:25-26)

The course Dr. Norton was teaching was titled *Living Word, Written Word*. The central text was Luke 24, the resurrection chapter. It's special because Jesus, the *logos*, (God's eternal living word) brings *rhema* (God's spoken word, living and active today) by explaining the *graphe* (written Scriptures of the Old Testament), revealing the truth about the Christ.

This truth is the core of the Gospel: Jesus, the Christ, would suffer, be crucified, and be raised from the dead. The two traveling men, the disciples, and the women at the tomb certainly knew he suffered, was crucified, and buried, but not resurrected. Somehow, they missed this theme in the Old Testament Scriptures, which Jesus filled the seven-mile walk with the traveling men by highlighting: "Then beginning with Moses and with all the prophets, He explained to them the things concerning Himself in all the Scriptures." (Luke 24:27)

THE IMPORTANCE OF *THESE THINGS*

While most English translations soften the Greek with "O foolish men and slow of heart to believe . . ." Dr. Norton taught it straight: "'Fools!' gives the best sense of this word in context." A quick word study on the word used, *anoetos*, shows it could be translated "lacking normal intelligence; mindless; dense; exhibiting a lack of brains." Ouch!

I'm just like the two traveling men, slow of heart and slow to perceive. Fear and ignorance keep me from understanding what is truly important. I get bogged down with everyday life and its troubles and don't see the life-giving message of the Gospel—the message of salvation. That message— the fact that Jesus came to earth, died for my sin, and was resurrected—is the '*these things*' that all these Scriptures are talking about. Twelve times this phrase is used between Luke 24:9-48:

- 24:9b [the women] "reported all *these things* to the eleven . . ."
- 24:10b [women] "were telling *these things* to the apostles."
- 24:14 "they were talking with each other about all *these things* which had taken place."
- 24:18b [Cleopas] "Are you the only one . . . unaware of *these things* which have happen . . . ?" (NASB2020)
- 24:19a [Jesus] "*What things?*"
- 24:19b [The two] "*The things* about Jesus the Nazarene..."
- 24:21 ". . . it is the third day since *these things* happened."
- 24:26 [Jesus] "Was it not necessary for the Christ to suffer *these things* . . . ?"
- 24:27 [Jesus] ". . . explained to them *the things* concerning Himself in all the Scriptures."
- 24:36 "While they were telling *these things*, He Himself stood in their midst . . ."
- 24:44 [Jesus] "These are My words . . . I spoke . . . while . . . with you, that *all things* . . . written about Me . . . must be fulfilled."
- 24:48 [Jesus] "You are witnesses of *these things*."

Jesus's death was completely futile in the minds of the two travelers until He challenged their denial and confusion with two questions: "What *things?*" and "Was it not necessary for the Christ to suffer *these things?*"

Then Jesus explained clearly "these things." He spent the rest of the walk sharing *these things* with them—how He was sent to earth, died, and was resurrected to bring salvation. The two travelers were kept from recognizing Jesus for the entire walk. Only when he broke bread at their table did the lights go on, and they realized, "Were not our hearts burning within us while He was speaking to us on the road, while He was explaining the Scriptures to us?" (Luke 24:32)

This is the message of the Gospel breaking through for the slow: Jesus is the eternal living word, *logos* (24:44), coming with the timely word, *rhema* (24:8), and illuminating the written word, *graphe*, to the travelers. He did this so they could live in resurrection and give witness to *these things*. (Luke 24:48-49)

But the travelers' slowness to recognize God showing up is painful. When God shows up in our own lives, how are we to know that He did? Like Jacob, after God visited him in a dream, said, "Surely the LORD is in this place, and I did not know it." (Genesis 28:16)

I'm not used to Jesus showing up unseen to speak directions, even when I ask for it. But He is patient with my density. He's breaking through my agnosticism—the fear that says that I don't know if it's His voice.

HEARING HIS VOICE CLEARLY

For a season, we attended a small neighborhood church because of its relationship to the refugee community and other community outliers, including a man needing to get his feet under him, who was living in the part-time pastor's office. Henry lived a life in and out of prison but was discovering life in Jesus through this community. Henry reciprocated by working on the elderly ladies' vehicles, changing their brakes and oil, etc.

One weekend, I was selling our 2000 Suburban, a vehicle gifted to Pam and me many years prior. I asked, "Lord, what do you want me to do with this vehicle?" It was in great shape and a good value for the right person, but it had been a gift. I didn't know if I should sell it, loan it, or donate it like we had done for a refugee family some years prior. I'd prayed about it for several months. With no clear answer, I listed it on Craigslist one Friday afternoon and got a surprisingly lackluster response. Sunday morning, I was speaking with Henry, and while he was telling me a story, I heard in my mind's ear a clear message: "Give the Suburban to Henry."

"What?" I asked. I almost said it out loud because the message was so extraordinary and surprising. It was disruptive, and didn't know if I could trust it, but it could be God. This had happened a couple of times prior, but I wasn't used to it. However, I had been praying about this. I pulled the pastor and another friend helping Henry aside and told them what happened. "You men know Henry best. Would you confirm this is a good idea?"

"This is great," they responded, and we arranged for the gifting.

Pulling into the parking lot of the church a few days later, I stuck my left arm out the window and plopped a big red bow on top of the Suburban. Henry watched with curious suspicion.

I got out of the car and walked over to Henry, grinning. "There's an interesting story behind this Suburban," I told him. "It was gifted to Pam and me a few years ago, but it really belongs to God. We have been stewards of it, and it's served our family well. We don't need this car anymore, so I asked God, 'What do You want us to do with Your Suburban?' Sunday, He told me to offer it to you as a gift, making you the new steward, if you will receive it. Pastor Joe and Chris affirmed this notion. We know this is a vehicle you can work on to keep in good repair, rely on to get to work while you get your feet under you financially, and carry your tools in it to help the elderly ladies when repairing their cars."

Henry's eyes began to brim. He was a hard man, but the gift of grace and entrustment hit a part of his heart no one could have imagined.

I got a hug from the hard guy. "No one has ever done anything like this for me," he said. The next Sunday, he shared the story with his new church family, emphasizing the gift of God's grace. Two years later, still fresh in his mind, he commented that the Suburban was the most tangible testimony of God's grace he'd ever experienced.

The most important thing about the most important person in the universe is He wants a two-way, life-giving conversation and friendship with us. How do we move beyond our slowness to perceive and learn to recognize His voice in all of life? In each subsequent chapter, we will add another stone to our wall of understanding.

ASK. THIS. NOW.

Three Tools for Learning to Hear God's Voice Using the 10-S Indicators

PERSONAL REFLECTION AND GROUP DISCUSSION

Do you have a story about being in the presence of someone important, well known, or powerful and without knowing it?

How might Luke 24 affect a person who says, "I only hear Jesus through Scripture"? I don't want to minimize the importance of Scripture, but consider my previous statement: It's special because Jesus, the *logos*, (God's eternal living word) brings *rhema* (God's spoken word, living and active today) by explaining the *graphe* (written Scriptures of the Old Testament), revealing the truth about the Christ.

How are the two disciples on the Emmaus Road like Jacob in Genesis 28:16 when he said, "Surely the Lord is in this place and I did not know it"? What contributes to your "slowness" to hear Jesus in the present?

10-S TEST

How many of the 10-S indicators of God's voice can you recall? Write down as many as you can.

_____   _____

_____   _____

_____   _____

_____   _____

Now flip to the Appendix (page 237) and read the succinct summary of how they are identified in the Luke 24 Emmaus Road Bible story and the story of Henry.

DISCUSS THIS QUESTION:

Which of the 10-S indicators of God's voice have you observed in your life story?

GIVE GOD A MINUTE JOURNAL

You Gotta *Ask*	You Gotta Listen & Watch *Answer*
Date:	

LAID BARE

How did Jesus help people overcome their barriers and see Him for who He really is—the Christ, Messiah-King? How does He speak to the individual about their real life and enter into their pain with them? And at what point does He speak through them to draw others into God's life?

When we are slow to perceive the identity and voice of Jesus, we miss out on the significance of things He is doing around us, to us, and through us. The previous chapter demonstrated different ways Jesus disrupted those closest to Him. This chapter tells the stories of how Jesus disrupted a Samaritan woman and me, breaking through our agnosticism, the doubt that we are actually hearing Him. These stories will help us see how He speaks to and through all kinds of people.

JESUS BREAKS THROUGH WITH THE SAMARITAN WOMAN

If the Samaritan woman's story is new to you, open a Bible and read John 4:3-42. Otherwise, if it's familiar, just read my summary of the conversation's high points illustrating how we can come to know we are hearing the voice of Jesus.

- John 4:3-7: Jesus shows up with a request as he is drawing water at noon, an unusual time when normal people are not doing this chore. The request is unusual: Jesus, a Jewish man (a rabbi), requesting a drink from an unclean Samaritan woman holding an unclean utensil. God's voice is **Surprising**.

- John 4:9-15: Jesus exposes her thirst for living water, eternal life. She asks, "Where then do you get that living water?" (4:11b) and says, "Sir, give me this water, so I will not be thirsty . . ." (4:15) Jesus gives a **Specific** answer to an ask.

- John 4:16-19: Jesus reveals the exact number of "husbands" she's had and that she doesn't currently have a husband. "Sir, I perceive that You are a prophet." (4:19) God's voice is **Smarter than you** and **Spot-on,** customized for the hearer.

- John 4:20-24: She seeks to dodge the truth by throwing out a theological division between Samaritans and Jews. Jesus points out foundational truths about worshipping God and the idea that salvation is from the Jews as unanimously underscored by the body of Jewish Scripture, which the Samaritan Torah came from. God's voice is **Scriptural.**

- John 4:25-26: She goes agnostic (believing she can't know) by deferring to a distant future Messiah. She's credited Jesus with being a prophet, so building on this, Jesus makes a startling revelation: "I who speak to you am He." God's voice often comes through to us in a **Succinct** one-liner.

- John 4:28-30: Leaving her waterpot, she went into the city, saying, "Come see a man who told me all the things that I have done; this is not the Christ, is it?" And people heard and came to Jesus. We know we've heard God's voice when it is **Spiritually fruitful.**

- John 4:8, 31-34: The disciples return and do not understand why Jesus is speaking with a Samaritan woman. They have food for Jesus, but he has more nourishment from the spiritual advancement. We confirm God's voice when it is **Supported by spiritually gifted people** and ultimately it is **Serving others' best interest.**

- John 4:35-42: A spiritual harvest happens among the Samaritans. "It is no longer because of what you said that we believe, for we have heard for ourselves and know that this One is indeed the Savior of the world." We know we've heard God's voice when it is **Salvation-minded.**

Who would ever have dreamed this woman would lead the men of her village to Jesus? God writes the most unlikely stories in our broken lives.

DREAMING OF DEER AND DAD

I had a similar experience. When packing for a men's retreat one fall, I felt a silent tap on my shoulder by the Holy Spirit: "You have unfinished business with a childhood story that you'll share at the Wild Courage men's retreat this weekend."

In the mountains, as we met for the first meeting of the retreat, the big room was full of men who looked like they were posing for a *Duck Dynasty* magazine cover shoot: beards and camo galore. Retreat co-host and friend, Bryan Byrd, myself, and about five others were the only ones among 40 who didn't have facial hair.

At this men's retreat, we were all instructed not to share our occupations throughout the weekend, disarming comparison and making every man an equal. We were told, "You have a story the whole world needs to hear, but what is said this weekend stays here. This is a safe place."

After the joint session, each of us would have 90 minutes to share his story in four-person groups. One man opened the joint session with his story, modeling these values and vulnerability. It made us feel better about our stories because his contained every horrible thing that could happen to a man. At least I knew what my leading story would be, but I still felt vulnerable and diminished, being a mere participant and not a leader. After all, leading conversations is what I do for my job, which I couldn't explain or even mention.

My friend Bryan is in law enforcement and does special investigations with occasional armed raids on bad guys. We've ministered side by side over the years, and he attends one of my men's groups when he is in town. Well into the evening, he stood up and said, "I have a gift for someone. Jon, would you come forward?"

It felt awkward being singled out, but he honored me as a mentor and said many kind things. He presented me with a replica of a two-edged sword used by a special-ops unit in World War II, telling the amazing story of the victory associated with it. I was delighted with this sword and humbled that he considered me a "special-ops" guy in the Kingdom. Neither of us had any idea how God would use this sword in my healing during the weekend.

Three real cowboys completed my foursome for my storytelling group. Doug was a typical cowhand, such as I grew up around, with a totally busted-up childhood. The other two, Grant and Britten, were nationally known, master horsehandlers. *This is curious*, I thought. *What are the odds I'd be with three real-deal cowboys to tell my story?* My dad was a cattle rancher, horse breeder, and racehorse trainer. This fact had a lot to do with my story. Britten, the West Texan, was our group guide.

I told my story, giving some life context about my parents' divorce at age 9 and being without my dad, who was on the road running horses 80 percent of the time. I shared about completing hunter safety training at age 10, and my heartbreak because my dad wasn't there to take me hunting like he did my older brothers—a fact he lamented. Along with hunting, I missed out on most of the cowboy training.

My throat was thick as I talked about how soon after passing my hunter's safety course, Dad, who was not present, sent me a rifle and a knife for Christmas. They sat in the closet, unused, for four years. The men listening to me were understanding, nodding as I continued the story of my brother finding the unused rifle and knife and chastising me.

Britten said, "Let's go back to your bedroom and replay in your mind's eye your brother finding the rifle and gun in the closet and how you responded to his words, 'Dad gave you this rifle and knife, and you don't even use them!' How did you feel when you heard this?"

I replied, "I was paralyzed and unable to speak. His words were true, but berating and soul-scorching. I felt unfairly judged and shamed, like I didn't have what it takes to be a hunter and therefore a man because I didn't have the ability and opportunity to use them. However, it was many years before I identified the emotion as shame. Compounding the effect was the fact that this brother was employed guiding hunters—and my dad had bought the rifle from him."

"Tell us what you'd say to him now if you were hearing his words through the ears of an adult," Britten prompted.

I felt the fire brim up within. Now a more articulate human at age 62, with emotional vocabulary under my belt, my words were raw and pointed. "Well, what the hell was I supposed to do? Get into a pickup I didn't own, with a driver's license I didn't have yet, and drive myself into a wilderness I didn't know to shoot down a big game animal with a rifle I didn't even know how to sight-in? Then would I gut it, cut it up, and pack it in my nonexistent pickup? What the #@%! are you talking about? You had someone to take you and train you. I have no one to go with."

The three cowboys sat quietly for a few moments until Britten asked, "Jon, picturing your old house, was there a safe place you could go to?"

"The wood pile. It's where I would go work out my angst and exhaust myself."

In my mind's eye, he had me walk out to the wood pile. There, I would come to terms with my feeling of being very alone.

"Jon, was your dad good with an axe?"

"Absolutely. He worked in the woods for his brother-in-law for a while."

"Jon, did you ever cut wood with your dad?"

I didn't see that question coming. It cut deep because that was one of the things I always wanted to do with him. Uncontrolled sobbing followed, the three knowing cowboys, broken men themselves, sharing my pain.

"Jon, I want you to hold the sword Bryan gave you in your hand. Let's go back to the bedroom." I pick up the sword that I had laid by my chair the evening before and walked back in my mind's eye. "Open the closet door and crawl into it; then close the door." Then Britten said, "Now close your eyes and invite the Holy Spirit to give you a vision of Jesus."

What will happen here? I wondered. Trusting Britten, I invited the Holy Spirit to do just that. Into my mind I saw a vague face with a not-so-vague two-edged sword coming out of His mouth. I was quite surprised and told the cowboys what I saw. Then it occurred to me this was an image in the book of Revelation—used six times, I later researched. It was the sword of the Spirit, the Word of God, faithful, true, and victorious.

Words landed in my head, not from any human mouth but from the Holy Spirit: "With my sword, I'm cutting the power cord on those destructive words."

Hebrews 4:12 came to mind, a verse I'd memorized many years ago: "For the word of God is living and active and sharper than any two-edged sword, and piercing as far as the division of soul and spirit, of both joints and marrow, and able to judge the thoughts and intentions of the heart."

And then I realized I was holding a two-edged special-ops sword, providentially gifted by Bryan the previous evening. I felt laid bare, but free.

The next morning, Britten told the larger group his broken story. Then he said, "I have some gifts to give. Jon, would you come up here? I wanted to retrieve this when you told your story yesterday. Before coming to the retreat, God put on my mind to purchase this axe handle, but I had no idea who it was for or why. I had you hold the sword during your story because the axe handle was in my room. It was clearly for you."

I was flooded with the kindness and wisdom of God putting this together, custom-fit for me. He not only provided a two-edged sword to clearly illustrate what He wanted me to learn, but also a second illustrated tool—an axe handle. I wrote in my journal, "Power cord cut on the shaming words that have chained me to hurt and pain. I'm being 'tooled-up,' holding two new tools to run special ops as a freedom fighter for other men."

NOTHING HIDDEN

Following Hebrews 4:12, where Paul talks about the two-edged sword, is verse 13: "And there is no creature hidden from His sight, but all things are open and laid bare to the eyes of Him with whom we have to do."

Just as Jesus opened the shame of the Samaritan woman, he opened mine. And, dramatically, he laid bare the other 40 men that weekend. At each meeting and on into the night, I heard sobbing throughout the building as men told their stories. Jesus, the healer Messiah, knows every square inch of us and our stories. He knows how to enter and creatively speak to our pain points with spot-on precision, truth, and compassion.

God has been speaking to all kinds of people all their lives, but so many haven't learned to hear His voice. They've not been invited to or taught how.

ASK. THIS. NOW.

PERSONAL REFLECTION AND GROUP DISCUSSION

You're becoming increasingly acquainted with the 10-S checklist of hearing God's voice. You observed all 10 of these in the Samaritan woman's encounter with Jesus in John 4. Take a minute to reflect on and recall how they are seen in John 4. Write comments next to them.

It's likely God speaking when it is . . .

1. Scriptural _____

2. Smarter than you _____

3. Surprising ("What?") _____

4. Specific (answer to an ask) _____

5. Succinct (one-liner) _____

6. Spot-on (customized) _____

7. Spiritually fruitful _____

8. Supported by spiritually gifted people _____

9. Salvation-minded _____

10. Serving others' best interests _____

Do you have a story about God revealing something about you that only He could have known? How did you react to this? Did you hide in shame, feel guilt, feel fear, feel loved, feel peace, feel joy, become an outspoken evangelist, or something else?

Appendix: 10-S Answer Key (page 238)

Test your memory and observations against the 10-S indicators of God's voice in the Appendix. Are there any surprises or insights gleaned from the Samaritan woman's exchange with Jesus?

How does this John 4 story support the subtitle of this book, *Jesus Is Speaking to and Through All Kinds of People*?

GIVE GOD A MINUTE JOURNAL

You Gotta *Ask*	You Gotta Listen & Watch *Answer*
Date:	

YOU CAN TRUST THAT GOD IS SPEAKING

Mark 13:11-13 says, ". . . do not worry beforehand what you are to say, but say whatever is given you in that hour; for it is not you who speak, but it is the Holy Spirit."

Remember that Jesus is speaking to and through all kinds of people. Who would have thought the Samaritan woman, talked about in the previous chapter, would become the lead evangelist to reach her Samaritan city? "Come, see a man who told me all things I have done; this is not the Christ, is it?" (John 4:29) She even connected a compelling question to her storyline, inviting others to look into this odd thing.

John 10:16 says, "I have other sheep . . . I must bring them also, and they will hear My voice and they will become one flock with one shepherd." This is an expansion from the disciple's original mission of reaching only the lost sheep of Israel. (Matthew 10:5-6) Like the Samaritan woman and her village, we are in the "other sheep" category. "They shall hear" is a future indicative (statement of fact) verb. Jesus tells us explicitly that He is speaking to people like the Samaritan woman, an unexpected participant. We may be surprised to learn He has been speaking to someone for a long time—maybe their whole life. He was there before we came on the scene. He will be there after we depart.

THE TRIANGLE OF COMMUNICATION

With this in mind, we need to remember that when talking to others about spiritual matters, there is a three-way discussion, similar to a triangle. We talk to God and He to us; God talks to the person—has been talking their whole life; and we talk to the person and they to us. It is a privilege to be included in the three-way discussion: us with the person, God with the person, and us with God. "... you will receive power when the Holy Spirit has come upon you; and you shall be my witnesses . . ." Acts 1:8. He empowers, and He promises to give us the words.

THE IMPORTANCE OF TRUST

In this three-way conversation we are often tempted to pull over and "go agnostic," doubting and wondering how we can really know if He will speak to us. It feels out of our control, and we fear He won't show up in our minds and mouths when we're on the spot. Deep down, we are afraid we won't know what to say, say it right, or have the courage to say it at all.

But isn't this the Holy Spirit's role as teacher, helper, truth-teller, reminder, one who convicts, discloser/illuminator, and guide? (John 14:16-17, 26; 15:26-27; 16:7, 13-15) He is speaking and leads our thoughts in what we are to say, be, or do.

"When the Helper comes, whom I will send to you from the Father, that is the Spirit of truth, who proceeds from the Father, He will testify about Me, and you will testify also because you have been with Me from the beginning." (John 15:26-27)

Our job, as described in John 15, is to obey His commandments (14:21; 15:9-11), and His job is to cause us to ". . . go and bear fruit . . . that whatever you ask of the Father in My name, He may give to you." (John 15:16)

Abide, ask, listen, watch, and obey. We cannot do this on our own but we can with the Holy Spirit. How do we learn this? It is simple. We listen to what He has said and is saying while actively trusting Him in the moment. He is speaking to you all the time. Trust Him.

THE RIGHT QUESTION

I'm going to share a story that dramatically changed the way I approach encounters with the people God brings into my life. It led me to a pivot in the way I abide, listen, watch, ask, and obey.

A friend set me up to meet with her boss for lunch at Applebee's. He was a psychiatrist and had been asking her many God questions, and she felt uncomfortable responding for a couple of reasons. One, he was her boss. Two, she didn't feel equipped to deal with his questions at the level he was asking them. Knowing what she did about me, she knew that I loved meeting with people and asking and answering life and God questions in a relational way. She persuaded him to meet me for lunch.

Small talk is never small. It allows people to get to know one another on a safe level. It is the wading pool to take each other's temperature and acclimate before diving into deeper water. I'm accustomed to beginning a conversation with a stranger talking about news, weather, and sports. It is where I like to begin.

Unfortunately, seated in the center of the restaurant at a tall table, this gentleman skipped the small talk and jumped right in with an intense question. Then he asked another and another. I tried to slow things down and get to know him first, but he kept coming. It felt awkward. He was intense, and I was afraid of responding to his questions before getting some life context. And he kept adding questions to the queue, and I listened, wondering where to begin, or if he even wanted me to.

For a mental health professional, this is very strange, I thought. I ventured to offer one idea on one question he asked, and he immediately interrupted and shut me down. Then he continued demanding answers to his questions but provided no space for my response. It was very awkward. Plus, his intensity was being noticed by people sitting around us. *This is bizarre*, I thought. *What do I do? Oh, maybe I should ask God!*

Finally, I said a silent prayer. *Father, I don't know what to do with this guy. Where is he coming from? What should I do?*

I got a very clear answer, as though I heard it audibly. These clear words passed through my mind: "Ask him if he's ever had an experience with Me."

What? Was that You, Lord? I'd never asked someone that question before, but it was a great idea. *It must be You because I'd never have thought to ask this.*

He paused his barrage of questions when I interjected, "May I ask you a question?" He slowly nodded, waiting. "Have you ever had an experience with God?" I asked.

His head dropped, shoulders slumped. He sighed an emphatic, "Yes!" It was as if an invisible creature had snapped his neck. I was shocked.

"Would you be willing to tell me about it?"

He did. It changed our conversation completely, like night and day. God knew the perfect disrupter. He dumped a story out, but I could tell we didn't get to the darkest part of it. I made myself available for another meeting, but it never happened. This one meeting would conclude my role in his spiritual journey.

What was that? I wondered afterward.

LETTING GOD USE ME HOWEVER HE WANTS

Here's my best analysis: It seemed that I was representing God to him from the start. He knew how to put me on my heels and keep me there because he was guarding his heart. His anger and disappointment with God caused inflammation in his soul due to harm done to a child in his life. Spiritually, he had turned His back on God, deep down knowing he needed to do business with God. Finally, God said, "Enough!

I'm bringing my boy Jon to ask him the question that will reach his hurt and pain."

Why did it take me so long to ask for help? I am grateful that eventually I did. That one question was all God had for me that day. God was speaking to him long before our lunch and, I trust, long afterward. In the providentially arranged encounter, God gave me the words when I finally asked. Succinct, smart, spot-on, synced with Scripture, surprising, and serving the man's best interest. There was a platform set for spiritual fruit/godly effect and this man experiencing salvation and deliverance from himself, taking a next step toward the blessing of a connected life in God. God used his employee's spiritual gift of encouragement to set the meeting up.

God will give us the words we need. He said He would. But you gotta ask, and you gotta listen.

ASK. THIS. NOW.

PERSONAL REFLECTION AND GROUP DISCUSSION

Have you had an experience with God or thought you heard His voice? Recall the circumstances, message, and effect.

Have you ever shared this experience with someone? Who could you share it with?

Since you're becoming increasingly acquainted with the 10 S's of hearing God's voice, consider how many of them apply to your particular story. Put a checkmark by the number, then make a short comment explaining how it was in play.

It's likely God speaking when it is . . .

1. Scriptural _____

2. Smarter than you _____

3. Surprising ("What?") _____

4. Specific (answer to an ask) _____

5. Succinct (one-liner) _____

6. Spot-on (customized) _____

7. Spiritually fruitful _____

8. Supported by spiritually gifted people _____

9. Salvation-minded _____

10. Serving others' best interests _____

If you've shared your faith with someone, have you ever asked God what to do or to give you the words? What happened?

If you felt it a failure, have you ever thought to ask, "God, what do I need to know about this experience?" Listen.

Appendix: 10-S Answer Key (page 239)

Consider Jon's story of the psychiatrist at Applebee's and ponder the Biblical support for asking God for words. You can start with Mark 13:11, but what else comes to mind?

Now, visit the Appendix and look for chapter 4, You Can Trust That God Is Speaking. What support is there for the 10-S indicators?

GIVE GOD A MINUTE JOURNAL

You Gotta *Ask*	You Gotta Listen & Watch *Answer*
Date:	

5

THE CONSEQUENCES OF OBEYING

In the city of Damascus many years ago, there was a man named Ananias. One day, he had a vivid dream where a voice called out to him, "Ananias!"

He replied, "Yes?"

The voice instructed, "There's a house on Straight Street. Go there and look for a man named Saul from Tarsus. He's praying right now, and in his own dream, he's seen you come and heal his blindness."

Ananias hesitated. "I've heard about this Saul. He's notorious for his actions against our community in Jerusalem. He even has permission from the religious leaders to arrest anyone who follows our beliefs."

But the voice insisted, "Trust me. Saul is important. He's going to share our message with not only the local people but also far-reaching nations and their leaders. And he will face many challenges for this cause."

So, Ananias, filled with a mix of apprehension and faith, went to the house. He found Saul and said, "Saul, I've been sent by the same voice you heard on your journey. I'm here to help you see again and to introduce you to the deeper mysteries."

As Ananias laid his hands on him, it was as if a veil was lifted from Saul's eyes. He could see! Elated and grateful, Saul was baptized, ate some food, and regained his strength.

Over the next few days, Saul, once a fierce opponent, began sharing in Damascus that the divine teachings were true. People were shocked. They said, "Isn't this the guy who was creating chaos in Jerusalem? The one against our community? Why is he now speaking on our behalf?"

But Saul, with his newfound passion, continued to grow in his convictions, astounding many by showcasing the depth and truth of the teachings.

JESUS SPEAKS TO AND THROUGH ALL KINDS OF PEOPLE

Fortunately, Ananias listened to God and obeyed the voice to visit Saul of Tarsus to lay hands on him and pray for him. Saul was no ordinary Jew. He had given hearty approval to the death by stoning of the first martyr, Stephen, (Acts 7) and continued to persecute many followers of Jesus.

After his conversion, Saul would be renamed Paul, the apostle. Perhaps it helped Ananias, who had very good reason to fear and second-guess the voice, to know "he is a chosen instrument of Mine, to bear My name before the Gentiles and kings and the sons of Israel; for I will show him how much he must suffer for My name's sake." (Acts 9:15)

Would it have helped if Ananias could look into the future and see a New Testament with Saul/Paul's name on two-thirds of its content? Or see that Saul/Paul would suffer all kinds of physical, social, and spiritual abuse, including false accusations, imprisonment, and martyrdom by beheading? Likely. But his role was to listen to God, obey, and trust God to work His sovereign plan for the world and individual lives. God told him, "Do specifically what I asked, Ananias."

HOPE IN THE FACE OF HARDSHIPS

God sharing with Ananias His intention for Paul gives all of us hope in the face of possible rejection, hardship, and persecution. I didn't mention these very real possibilities in the previous chapter because we need to think of one challenge at a time. First, He will give us the words when we need them. Second, it may cost you to deliver the words, but the eternal reward well exceeds the cost.

Jesus warned the 12 disciples about the cost of bearing witness of Christ. "But be on your guard; for they will deliver you to the courts, and you will be flogged in the synagogues, and you will stand before governors and kings for My sake, as a testimony to them. The Gospel must first be preached to all the nations. When they arrest you and hand you over, do not worry beforehand about what you are to say, but say whatever is given you in that hour; for it is not you who speak, but it is the Holy Spirit. Brother will betray brother to death, and a father his child; and children will rise up against parents and have them put to death. You will be hated by all because of My name, but the one who endures to the end, he will be saved." Mark 13:9-13

God has always wanted us to hear and respond, listen and obey. God is good, and it's all for something great, glorious, and permanent. It's possible we don't hear God so well for fear of the cost. "I am not courageous," we tell ourselves.

FEARING THE RIGHT THING

At a Jordan Peterson speaking event, a guest wrote this question: "How are you so brave in the face of the cultural and political pounding you take from people and even your own government [Canada]?"

He quickly fired back, "I'm not brave! I'm just afraid of the right thing." He was implying that God and Truth are the "right thing" in the context of his message.

What do we ultimately fear? Jesus said, "Do not fear those who kill the body but are unable to kill the soul; but rather fear Him who is able to destroy both soul and body in hell." (Matthew 10:28)

What do we ultimately love? He invites us to count the cost of loving Him above our closest family relationships, our own lives, and the things we possess. (Luke 14:25-35) If we love Him ultimately, we hear His voice and keep His commandments. (John 14:21)

If we don't settle on what the most important thing is in our lives, we stay in the realm of self-preservation and self-promotion. We won't hear His voice or keep His commandments, especially taking a stand with Him publicly. Situations force us to choose what is ultimate and whether we will listen and obey or not.

THE RESULTS OF OBEDIENCE

Eric Fredriksen was at CrossFit in the midst of a workout when he heard a voice in his mind's ear say, "Invite Haps to the men's group."

"What? No! Wait . . . is that you, Lord?" Eric reasoned, "Certainly God knows Chris 'Haps' Hapner is a hard and even sarcastic skeptic when it comes to God and a little intimidating to many of the CrossFitters." He pushed the message to the side, but it came again—more urgently.

"Invite Chris Hapner to the men's group." Eric began to soften toward God, but was still fearful.

"Okay, Lord, if this is you, I'll do it." Instead of stalling or trying to talk himself out of it, he just blurted it out because Haps was right next to him.

"Haps, do you know about our men's group that meets on Tuesday mornings?"

"Yes."

"Well, why don't you come?"

"I'd love to."

Eric was stunned. No mocking or inquisition. Just an affirmative. He wasn't expecting this at all. Now it was code red to warn all the group members, "Haps said he's coming." Everyone knew Chris Hapner meant whatever he said, so they needed to be ready for him to be there.

A few days later, Haps attended the Tuesday meeting and participated in serious life and God discussions as if he had been doing it all his life. He loved it and the following week was even chiding another guy on the text thread who was trying to excuse himself from coming that week.

This is a group that practices hospitality to newcomers. And it's *Cheers* for the regulars: "Everybody knows your name and they're always glad you came." Each guy is celebrated and bombarded with cowboy love. The men are real and keep confidences. Haps felt right at home with the intelligent and authentic discussions.

"What is going on with Haps?" the men wondered. It was like one of the wonders of the world to have him in the room. He began attending in the midst of discussing our newly released book *You Gotta Ask*. He never missed group except when he was out of town. And he was always early.

One day, during the group, I asked him why he had changed and become open to discussing God and investigating life questions. I said, "You have a reputation with the guys of being an outspoken critic and skeptic. What's different?"

He didn't even have to think about it. He offered, "Something I heard Jordan Peterson say on a podcast. 'What you want most is where you least want to look.' In my case, I thought that this might be about God. I thought I should be more open to this. Then came Eric's invitation."

Some weeks after this, I asked Eric and Haps to replay the invitation and exactly what was going on in both of their minds when Eric invited Haps to the group. We were at a place where it would be educational to engage in this analysis.

Haps said, "Had Eric asked me one day sooner or two days later, I wouldn't have come."

"Really! Why?" I asked.

"I thought the guys were avoiding me on Tuesdays, the morning I coached at CrossFit. I was offended by this. And then I learned that they were not avoiding me but attending the men's group that morning. So offense was removed and my curiosity heightened. I like these guys, so of course, I wanted to check it out. But had I not been invited while it was fresh, I might have remained in my old ways. However, I told Eric I would come, so I did."

God knew this. It's why He was persistent with Eric in two strong back-to-back messages saying, "Invite Haps to the men's group."

We were reading through Mark's Gospel, then went on a discussion tangent when Haps chimed in, "I want to read the Bible." We learned he was sitting down with his wife and son, reading through the Bible together each week. They had started in Genesis and were trying to make sense of it. He would often come in asking tough questions like "Why did God command Abraham to sacrifice Isaac?"

"Do you have a Bible, Chris, or are you reading from an iPhone Bible app?" A few days after confirming that he had been using his Bible app, Chris was presented with a beefy leather-bound ESV study Bible. It was loaded with analysis and commentary from renowned Bible teachers. He was delighted. That week he sent a text picture of his 11-year-old son reading that Bible on his own initiative. So we sent another Bible home with Chris, the exact same one but a different color.

Soon after this, Chris got up to go to church for the first time one Sunday morning, and his wife confronted him. "Wait a minute. What's going on here? We always talk about everything. Tell me what's going on with you."

Chris has been with the men's group for almost two years now. I suspect he went home to have another conversation with her after this week's group, where some members decided to get baptized in the Boise River as believing adults to identify publicly with Jesus.

Lives are being changed because Eric listened to God to open his office to host a seeker's study and discussion. He listened to God to invite Chris Hapner, among several others, to the group. Haps is now inviting others to the group and into spiritual conversations.

ASK. THIS. NOW.

PERSONAL REFLECTION AND GROUP DISCUSSION

Things tend to work out beautifully when we hear God's voice and obey, trusting Him for results.

Ask God to bring to mind anyone He's been talking to you about to invite into a setting where they can take the next step toward God. Maybe it begins with an invitation to coffee or lunch to hear their story.

"Jesus, who should I pray for?" Who comes to mind? Make a list. Pray for them right now.

_____ _____

_____ _____

_____ _____

_____ _____

In the next chapter, we'll tell you about another man's list, developed when he heard God's voice in his mind's ear naming three men to pray for. Next, we'll look at how Jesus prayed for the lost and scattered sheep who would hear His voice. Finally, we'll discuss how Paul prayed for others who were spiritually lost as he was when he was Saul of Tarsus.

Have you had an experience with God like Eric or Ananias had—a persistent voice directing you to do the unimaginable? Perhaps you thought you heard His voice, but you tried to dismiss it. Recall the circumstances, message, and effect.

Review the 10 S's and put a checkmark by each one that relates. If you don't have a story like Ananias, use his story with Saul, writing a comment about how each was in play. Don't stress about getting them all.

It's likely God speaking when it is . . .

1. Scriptural _____

2. Smarter than you _____

3. Surprising ("What?") _____

4. Specific (answer to an ask) _____

5. Succinct (one-liner) _____

6. Spot-on (customized) _____

7. Spiritually fruitful _____

8. Supported by spiritually gifted people _____

9. Salvation-minded _____

10. Serving others' best interests _____

Appendix: 10-S Answer Key (page 240)

Take Ananias's story of God telling him to pray for Saul and Eric's story of inviting Chris to men's group and identify as many 10-S indicators as possible.

Now, visit the Appendix and look for chapter 5, The Consequences of Obeying. How many did you get?

Like Ananias, pray for people on your list. Pray for the scales to fall off their eyes, for Jesus's light to enlighten, and for them to be born of the Spirit and nourished with the bread of life. Also pray for open doors for you and others to share Jesus.

GIVE GOD A MINUTE JOURNAL

You Gotta *Ask*	You Gotta Listen & Watch *Answer*
Date:	

IF JESUS DID IT . . .

Is there anything more important in a relationship than listening? Is there anyone more important to listen to than God? Jesus only did what He saw the Father doing. He clearly told us that this was only possible by His asking and listening in prayer. They were working together. [Jesus] ". . . was calling God His own Father, making Himself equal with God." (John 5:17-18)

HOW MUCH MORE?

"Truly, truly, I say to you, the Son can do nothing of Himself, unless it is something He sees the Father doing; for whatever the Father does, these things the Son also does in like manner. For the Father loves the Son, and shows Him all things that He Himself is doing; and the Father will show Him greater works than these, so that you may marvel. For just as the Father raises the dead and gives them life, even so the Son also gives life to whom He wishes." (John 5:19-21)

We need to think long and hard about the phrase "how much more." If Jesus, who is God in the flesh, can do nothing of

Himself, how much more is that true of you and I? If Jesus only does what He sees and hears the Father doing, *how much more* do we need to know what God is saying and doing in order to do anything ourselves?

JESUS'S COMMANDS TO US

Jesus often went off to a mountain at night to pray—alone. Sometimes it preceded significant things, like the choosing of the 12 apostles (Luke 6:12-13). On another significant occasion, he brought Peter, James, and John, who would see Jesus transfigured in His glory. The message to them was similar to the one given at His baptism: "A voice came out of the cloud, saying, 'This is My Son, My Chosen One; listen to Him!'" (Luke 9:35)

"Listen to Him" uses a present tense imperative verb—a command to continually observe. Both Matthew in the sending of the 12 apostles to preach and minister healing (Matthew 9:35-10:2) and Luke in the sending of the 70 to do likewise (Luke 10:1-3, 9) include a command to pray for laborers: "The harvest is plentiful, but the workers are few. Therefore beseech the Lord of the harvest to send out laborers into His harvest." (Matthew 9:37b-38) They were sent in pairs to do mission in Jesus's name and authority.

His last words before His ascension into heaven were, "All authority has been given to me in heaven and on earth. Go therefore and make disciples of all the nations, baptizing . . . teaching them to observe all that I commanded you; and lo, I am with you always, even to the end of the age." (Matthew 28:18-20)

YOU GOTTA LISTEN

Remember that if we as sheep hear His voice, we have all authority to go in His name because He has all authority in heaven and earth. He is with us to the end as we obey His commands. He asks us to make disciples among all people groups while praying for more laborers.

In Matthew chapter 9, the tax collector Matthew, after showing Jesus's authority over everything (sin, physical illnesses and afflictions, demons, death, and men), commissions the reader to do the following:

- Go as Jesus went
- See as Jesus saw
- Feel compassion as Jesus felt compassion
- Proclaim the good news and minister to people's needs as Jesus did
- Pray as Jesus prayed

START WHERE YOU ARE

Luke adds these last words from Jesus before His ascension: "But you will receive power when the Holy Spirit has come upon you; and you shall be my witnesses . . . in Jerusalem . . ." (Acts 1:8)

The disciples were in Jerusalem and they were to start where they were. This is what Tony Ball did. At a huge men's conference, Promise Keepers, he was invited to pray for people in his life circle who didn't know Jesus yet. So Tony asked God to bring to mind whom he should pray for. As He listened, three faces came into his mind's eye. He prayed for these three men and wrote their names on a bookmark, intended to be a prayer prompt going forward. One was his father, Howard; one was a client, Griz; and one was a neighbor, Doug.

A few years later, Tony invited me to meet with his neighbor, Doug, to field some challenging questions about God, Jesus, and the Bible. Doug had an analytical mind and was willing to systematically power through his great questions. We began meeting every two weeks for breakfast to explore these and to discuss his life journey. A great friendship developed.

These meetings with Doug went on for several months into the spring, when I also met Griz at our church's men's retreat. Griz, by his own admission, was a burned-out drug addict. At the retreat, Griz met Jesus. A few weeks later he died.

I also met Howard who moved to Boise, Idaho, that year to be closer to Tony and his family. Tony invited Howard to church. That summer, the Luis Palau Festival occurred, a community-wide outreach in the greater Boise area. There was a strong prayer emphasis among the participating churches. Howard went forward to make his peace with Jesus.

This same summer, Doug told me he was ready to make Jesus his Savior and Lord. He demonstrated his new faith through agreeing to be baptized in the frigid Boise River.

Right before Doug's baptism, I received a call from Tony. I could hear the enthusiasm abounding in his voice. "You will never guess what I just found in my desk drawer. A book marker with three names on it to be prayed for: Dad, Griz, and Doug. I completely forgot about it after filling the names in several years ago at the Promise Keepers conference. It's unbelievable that I would find it *right now*, during the same summer all three men would come to know Jesus! I think God wanted me to see this to be encouraged that He is faithful."

No doubt. You gotta ask. You gotta listen.

ASK. THIS. NOW.

PERSONAL REFLECTION AND GROUP DISCUSSION

How does the Tony Ball story inspire you? What percentage of Jesus-followers practiced these two simple acts as a way of life: praying for people by name and inviting them to opportunities to hear about Jesus?

You know what to do. If you have names to add to your list from chapter 5, prayerfully do so, asking God to bring people to mind to pray for. (Neighbors, co-workers, family members, recreation friends.) Who needs to take the next step toward Jesus, starting with us interceding for them at the throne of grace? They may be among whom Jesus meant when He said, "I have other sheep . . . I must bring them also, and they will hear My voice . . ." (John 10:16)

1.

2.

3.

Appendix: 10-S Answer Key (page 241)

In the chapter 6 section of the Appendix, you will have opportunity to scan or delve into the 10-S indicators, seeing the voice of Jesus in action, praying as Jesus prayed and going as Jesus went.

Whether reading on your **own** or discussing as a group, read through the 10 S's out loud, then turn to the Appendix, chapter 6.

It's likely God speaking when it is . . .

1. Scriptural _____

2. Smarter than you _____

3. Surprising ("What?") _____

4. Specific (answer to an ask) _____

5. Succinct (one-liner) _____

6. Spot-on (customized) _____

7. Spiritually fruitful _____

8. Supported by spiritually **gifted** people _____

9. Salvation-minded _____

10. Serving others' best interests _____

GIVE GOD A MINUTE JOURNAL

You Gotta *Ask*	You Gotta Listen & Watch *Answer*
Date:	

GOD IS BIGGER THAN INJUSTICE

One day my friend Steve McCormick told me, "You need to meet my friend Keith. He's a retired Navy SEAL medic. I want to get you guys set up for lunch." A few days later, in a completely different conversation with another friend, Kyle Cammack, Keith was mentioned again: "You need to meet Keith Barry. I told him he needed to meet you." After that, I was excited to meet Keith and curious about what I would discover, given two friends initiated this introduction.

INJUSTICE

Keith and I met for lunch twice in the next few weeks. As I sat listening to him, I am fairly certain that his story impacted me more than I impacted him. He was in Boise, engaging in two intensive courses to find direction for his life. What does a Navy SEAL medic do next? His effective life-saving tactics in combat were not suitable for becoming an ER doctor. This is common for special forces operators—specially trained and highly tactile with high performance, high adrenaline, amazing experiences, and unmatched comradery with their "band of brothers" who lived with high stress, trauma, and loss. They are indeed special people. But then what?

Over barbeque, Keith told me how he'd had a sense of calling to be a SEAL medic from a young age. "You can Google my name and read much of what I'm going to tell you," he said. The story that you would read is about his three-year imprisonment resulting from an accusation of raping a woman whom he dated and broke up with. The accusation came after the break-up. It was during the #MeToo period in our country when the mere accusation was assumed to be true.

"In the military during this time, you were guilty until proven innocent. Is this my payback for 19 years and 8 tours of distinguished service as a SEAL medic? By the time I was 35 years old, I had watched 43 people die." He didn't tell me how many lives he'd saved.

Both of our mutual friends, Steve and Kyle, mentioned sensing the trauma Keith experienced. The accusation and imprisonment with little hope of exoneration in three years created trauma upon trauma. Then an officer read his case file and started pressing the issue within the bureaucracy about why Keith was still in prison without proof of guilt. Eventually, he was exonerated and given an honorable discharge.

After his discharge, Keith spent a long time raging at the injustice. He bought a Sprint van and headed for the mountains to get lost and work it out. He went off the grid and, during this time, experienced a dark night of the soul, entertaining dark thoughts to match.

Having prayed about this lunch encounter, God put in my mind to ask Keith a question that, until recently, I'd not asked much. "I'm curious about your spiritual journey. I have an unusual question. Have you ever had an experience with God or thought you heard God's voice?"

YOU ARE NOT GOING TO QUIT

A smile crawled over Keith's face, and he recounted two different scenarios, years apart.

The first was during Navy SEAL training when, legs trembling from exhaustion, he and several trainees were carrying a rubber boat over their heads. A training officer got in his face, screaming, "You're not going to quit."

He recounted, "This struck me as very odd, as they were always trying to break us and get us to quit." Only a handful of the hundred or so recruits would become SEALs.

"Here's the thing," he said. "I was not the smartest or strongest guy, the best athlete or the toughest guy. I had to do a workaround, joining the Marines instead of the Navy just to be admitted into the program, and maybe it was because I wanted to be a SEAL medic that I made it. Their agenda was to thin us out and eliminate the majority. It was unusual that I made it in, survived it, and heard the message, 'You're not going to quit!' I believe God intended for me to become a SEAL medic because everything about me becoming one was against all odds."

The second experience was during the dark night in the Sprint van in the mountains. The indignity of "guilty until proven innocent," the compounded loss of three years from imprisonment, the end of a career, and not knowing what was next led to a dark place. Without giving you the details about what he was thinking of doing, he heard during this hard time the same very specific words, "You're not going to quit."

HEAR HIS VOICE

God is speaking to and through all kinds of people throughout their lives. But we don't know His voice. "I have other sheep . . . I must bring them also, and they will hear My voice . . ." (John 10:16)

It's almost as if Jesus was standing outside Keith's Sprint van's sliding door saying, "Behold, [Hey, listen up!] I stand at the door and knock; if anyone hears My voice and opens the door, I will come in to him, and will dine with him, and he with Me." (Revelation 3:20)

"You're not going to quit," was an invitation to life and dinner with the Good Shepherd, who has always been there. Like Jacob, in a nanosecond, Keith realized a connection between the first message and the second. "Surely, the Lord is in this place, and I did not know it." (Gen 28:16) A lost and scattered sheep, Keith became aware that the Good Shepherd was there and had been a long time. He was speaking to him.

THE COMFORTING WORDS OF DAVID

Psalm 23 is arguably one of the most recognized Scriptures in the Bible. People may not be able to quote all six verses verbatim, but they know almost all of them. It's quoted and read in hard times, especially around the death of loved ones. It's a warm, dark-time Psalm. It belongs to everyone, including the lost, scattered, and threatened sheep. The chapter flows from warm to dark to surprise!

PSALM 23:1-6

Verses 1-3 are the warm part:

> *The Lord is my shepherd,*
> *I shall not want.*
> *He makes me lie down in green pastures;*
> *He leads me beside quiet waters.*
> *He restores my soul;*
> *He guides me in the paths of righteousness*
> *For His name's sake.*

Verse 4 is the dark part, but He's with us:

> *Even though I walk through the valley of the shadow of death,*
> *I fear no evil, for You are with me;*
> *Your rod and Your staff, they comfort me.*

Verse 5 is the surprising part:

> *You prepare a table before me in the presence of my enemies;*
> *You have anointed my head with oil;*
> *My cup overflows.*

Surprise! What is the last verse doing here? What does it have to do with sheep? Isn't this a non sequitur? Why the mixing of metaphors? First we see a lone sheep moving through a deep, dark, hot canyon, threatened by natural and predatory "enemies." All at once he discovers himself to be the honored guest of God, a table of bountiful food and drink with the pleasure and nurture of oil applied to the parched scalp. It's a beautiful picture of hospitality.

Verse 6 is the greatest part—it's permanent:

> *Surely goodness and lovingkindness will follow me all the days of my life,*
> *And I will dwell in the house of the Lord forever.*

God has always been there. We need to listen for the warm and dark parts of another's story. Then watch for the surprising part where God invites them to dinner to shower them with relational connection, abundance, goodness, and lovingkindness forever.

ASK. THIS. NOW.

PERSONAL REFLECTION AND GROUP DISCUSSION

Jesus said, "I have other sheep . . . I must bring them also, and they will hear My voice . . ." (John 10:16) How does Keith's life story illustrate the subtitle of this book, *Jesus Is Speaking to and Through All Kinds of People*?

Psalm 23 illustrates how God uses the valley of the shadow of death (Psalm 23:4), the darkness we experience in our pain and pressure points, to prepare us for the table of abundance He has prepared for us in the presence of our enemies—anything threatening our life. (Psalm 23:5) How are darkness, pain, and pressure beneficial in helping us hear God?

Keith intuitively knew it was God's voice because it was so distinctive. He simply needed someone to affirm this and to invite him to take the next step. Are there more "Keiths" out there around you? Consider the 10 S's of Keith hearing God's voice below.

Appendix: 10-S Answer Key (page 242)

To reflect on and answer some of the questions above, you may want to visit the chapter 7 section of the Appendix to explore the voice of Jesus, the Good Shepherd, in Psalm 23 and what it looks like in Keith's story. You will see there is a case for all 10.

It's likely God speaking when it is . . .

1. Scriptural _____
2. Smarter than you _____
3. Surprising ("What?") _____
4. Specific (answer to an ask) _____
5. Succinct (one-liner) _____
6. Spot-on (customized) _____
7. Spiritually fruitful _____
8. Supported by spiritually gifted people ____
9. Salvation-minded _____
10. Serving others' best interests _____

TAKE THE CHALLENGE

Who will take the challenge to do as Jon did? Ask someone this question:

"I'm curious, has there ever been a time when you thought you experienced God or heard God's voice?"

You could tell them the story of Keith or your own story, if they're curious.

PRAY

"Father, bring someone to mind or cause my path to cross with someone I can ask this question."

GIVE GOD A MINUTE JOURNAL

You Gotta *Ask*	You Gotta Listen & Watch *Answer*
Date:	

THE THREE BARRIERS TO COMMUNICATING WITH CHRIST

You gotta listen because Jesus is speaking to and through all kinds of people. This chapter addresses three things that get in the way of this.

BARRIER ONE

The first barrier that gets in the way of our witness for Christ is that we are uncomfortable with the notion that God speaks to people, Spirit to spirit. We are taught that hearing voices in our heads seems suspect. As comedian Lily Tomlin asked, "Why is it that when we speak to God, we are said to be praying, but when God speaks to us, we are said to be schizophrenic?"

BARRIER TWO

The second barrier we encounter is an agnosticism about how God speaks. We think it's our responsibility to persuade others and be brilliant, all the time underestimating that God is already speaking to people in many creative and customized ways.

BARRIER THREE

The third barrier is that, like the Corinthians, we have a faulty understanding of what is valuable and what makes us valuable. We accumulate masks, or false selves, through which we seek to find our lives. These accumulate under the banners of wisdom, beauty, power, influence, wealth, and health. All of these things are good but get distorted by pride (false appraisal of ourselves) and diminish our God-given identities.

Paul disrupts the Corinthians on all three fronts in his two letters to them.

FIRST, DOES GOD SPEAK TO US SPIRIT TO SPIRIT?

Being God's image-bearers, we are "hardwired" to hear God's voice. Being born again and dwelt within by the Holy Spirit, we are "software-installed" to run life applications such as dialogue with the Triune God, receiving guidance and empowerment for service as well as witnessing and manifesting the fruit of the Spirit.

You may have noticed in the first few chapters the examples of hearing God's voice are largely God speaking to a person, Spirit to spirit, mixing spiritual thoughts with spiritual words. In each chapter we are teaching our minds to observe the 10-S characteristics common in Biblical and personal stories. With the 10-S characteristics, we are learning how to know it is God and not our own thoughts, the world's influence, or the evil one.

There may be some tension growing in you because of the stories shared in this book. You may be wondering if you can trust them. Understand that we are building a case for this being your normal life in Christ. If it feels subjective, like it exists within your own mind and consciousness, you are right. This is where learning to hear God starts for each of us. However, we must verify it, starting with comparing it to Jesus's words and Scripture—which claim to be the living and written Word of God.

Allow me to introduce you to another expert witness with unique qualifications. He shares our viewpoint about the authority of Scripture and the unique identity claims of Jesus to be the eternal Son of God.

PHENOMENOLOGY

The late Dr. Dallas Willard was a career philosophy professor at the University of Southern California (USC), including chairman of the department for several years. In the common secular state university experience, you would not expect a philosophy professor to espouse a viewpoint that God speaks to us through the Bible, let alone that God speaks to each of us through the Holy Spirit. But this is where Dr. Willard is fascinating, and it's why most Christian philosophers and many Christian leaders engage in reading and studying his books in the field of spiritual formation. (I hope you will become an equal fan of his generous and challenging writings.) Dr. Willard's expertise is in a branch of philosophy called phenomenology.

A quick-click on Wikipedia gives us a framework. "Phenomenology is the philosophical study of objectivity—and reality more generally—as subjectively lived and experienced. It seeks to investigate the universal features of consciousness while avoiding assumptions about the external world, aiming to describe phenomena as they appear to the subject, and to explore the meaning and significance of the lived experiences."

In his book *Hearing God: Developing a Conversational Relationship with God*, Dr. Willard outlined six ways God has communicated with us within the biblical record:

1. A phenomenon plus a voice, e.g., God, Moses, and a burning bush (Exodus 3:3-6)

2. A supernatural messenger or an angel, e.g., Gabriel and Mary (Luke 1:26-38)

3. Dreams and visions, e.g., Jacob (Genesis 28:11-17) and Peter (Acts 10:9-19)

4. An audible voice, e.g., Samuel (1 Samuel 3)

5. A human voice, e.g., God speaking through Moses (Exodus 4:12)

6. The human spirit; the "still, small voice," e.g., Elijah (1 Kings 19:12, KJV) and Paul (1 Corinthians 2:9-16)

Willard sees the sixth way God communicates, to the human spirit, like Elijah hearing the still, small voice as "the primary subjective way God addresses us." (*Hearing God*, p. 130) It is subjective in that it comes from within. He continues, ". . . it most engages the faculties of free, intelligent beings involved in the work of God as His co-laborers and friends." In 1 Corinthians 2:10-13, the Holy Spirit, resident in the believer, searches the depths of God and depths of a person communicating [Spirit to spirit] *"combining spiritual thoughts with spiritual words."* (1 Corinthians 2:13b) This means we can know the mind of God, Christ, and the Holy Spirit. "But we have the mind of Christ." (1 Corinthians 2:16b)

GOD'S RELATIONAL AND WARM WAY OF SPEAKING TO US

It's a good thing God speaks to us in more obscure ways so that He doesn't overwhelm us. The quiet reading of the Word, or the subjective Spirit-to-spirit communication, allows us space and time to respond. This is superior to the Greeks (or anyone) searching for wisdom (1 Corinthians 2:1-8) or Jews seeking signs (1 Corinthians 1:22; 1:18-2:9) because it's relational, warm, and forward-moving.

Willard writes, "We get beyond the need to have big things [signs and wonders] happening to reassure us that somehow we are all right . . . Then we begin to understand that God's whole purpose is to bring us to the point where he can walk with us quietly, calmly and constantly, leaving us space to grow to be his (often fumbling) co-laborers . . . Even at the merely human level, one of the highest forms of communication in which no overt word is needed or wanted." (*Hearing God*, pp. 151-152)

ONE OF THE HIGHEST FORMS OF COMMUNICATION

Paul, recounting for the Corinthians their salvation story, reminded them that he came in weakness and fear, trembling—not like the eloquent showman they were used to hearing in the public square. He came with no shock and awe, no Garth Brooks or Tony Robbins, and no signs and wonders. Instead, his power was in the simplicity of the Gospel of Christ, crucified and risen, confirmed through the power of the Holy Spirit, revealing and illuminating their spirits in the unseen spaces of their souls.

There is nothing in the observable human realm to explain the Corinthians' conversion to Christ. Nothing. As Christ-followers and Christ-witnesses, we need to get this. It's how it started and how it still works today. So appraise all things and people with the mind of Christ, knowing that it's God who causes the growth, Spirit to spirits. (1 Corinthians 2:14-3:7)

SECOND, ARE WE BRAVE ENOUGH TO STEP OUT AND OBEY?

Observing how God spoke to the Corinthians helps us overcome our fear to witness for Christ. You may feel like you don't know enough or won't speak well enough to witness to others. But note how the 10-S characteristics of hearing God's voice are present in Paul's recounting of the Corinthians coming to faith and their growth in Christ. If you read 1 Corinthians 1:18-3:15, you get a clear impression of how Paul came in weakness and fear. However, he had God's power to speak, Spirit to human spirit. And you do too.

- **Synced with Scripture**: e.g., in the first three chapters of 1 Corinthians, reminding them of how God revealed Himself through Paul to them he liberally quotes Old Testament Scripture such as Isaiah 64:4; 65:17 in 1 Corinthians 2:9 and Isaiah 40:13 in 1 Corinthians 2:16.

- **Smarter than you**: e.g., in 1 Corinthians 1:29-30, Paul says God is wiser than the Corinthians, " . . . so that no man may boast before God. But by His doing you are in Christ Jesus . . ."

- **Surprising**: Even Paul the scholar says to the self-wise Corinthians, "I determined to know nothing among you except Jesus Christ and Him crucified." (1 Corinthians 2:2)

- **Specific (answer to prayer)**: Acts 18:9-10, God spoke to Paul in a night vision to keep on speaking to the Corinthians resulting in their conversion, by God's power. (1 Corinthians 2:1-5)

- **Succinct**: God encouraged Paul, ". . . go on speaking [to the then unconverted and hostile Corinthians] and do not be silent; for I am with you . . . I have many people in this city." (Acts 18:9-10)

- **Spot-on**: Read 1 Corinthians 1:18-31 to enjoy how customized God's simple and powerful message through Paul was for the Corinthians, choosing the foolish/weak to shame the wise/strong.

- **Spiritually fruitful**: Paul reminds the Corinthians, "But by His [God's] doing you are in Christ Jesus" (1:30) and "God was causing the growth . . ." (1 Corinthians 3:6b (7b))

- **Supported by spiritually gifted people**: In the spiritual growth God caused, he used God-gifted evangelists/teachers like Paul and Apollos. "I planted, Apollos watered . . . God was causing the growth . . ." (1 Corinthians 3:6)

- **Salvation-minded**: God's speaking to us often relates to people coming to know Him. While the Corinthians were hostile to Paul and the Gospel, God encouraged him, ". . . go on speaking . . . I have many people in this city [who will come to know Me]." (see Acts 18:9-10) Paul summarizes: ". . . by His [God's] doing you are in Christ Jesus . . . righteousness . . . sanctification, and redemption." (1 Corinthians 1:30)

- **Serving others' best interests**: Sharing the Gospel with the prideful Corinthians was full of hardship. Conversion (Acts 18:1-18) through bringing them into maturity in Christ was a hardship. (Read 1 and 2 Corinthians to appreciate the hardship on Paul.)

Bill Bright taught us with precision: "We share Christ in the power of the Holy Spirit, leaving the results to God."

THIRD, IS YOUR FALSE SELF KEEPING YOU FROM HEARING GOD?

Like the Corinthians, we have a faulty appraisal of what is valuable and what makes us valuable. Our hearts, apart from the true God, are idol-making factories. We accumulate masks, or false selves, to self-promote and self-preserve, which leads to competition, division, separation, and cancellation.

HUMILIATION AT THE SENATE

For several years, at the invitation of an Idaho legislator, I've led a weekly Bible study with legislators during a three-month legislative session. Though I have always had a geeky political interest since grade school, I am not politically partisan in this role. I enter the Senate majority caucus room as a "Jesus-Kingdom guy" focused on building the eternal Kingdom that transcends temporary—but God-ordained—government.

Politics is a ruthless dogfight, pitting anyone against anyone on a given day or season. This particular year was loaded with strife. There was concern about people's motivations being relational and political more than doing what was best for the state. This created some awkwardness for legislators about what to support.

Our attendance dropped a bit, but our discussions were still quality. One week was especially disappointing because our attendance was quite low, but I was enthused about the text. In the midst of the discussion, a key participant jumped up and said, "I have to go." Shortly after, another key participant did the same, leaving us with only a small handful of people. Though it was awkward for me, it ended up being a good discussion. However, at the end, I slinked out the door thinking, *I think my time is done here. This is failing.*

From the top floor of the Capitol to the sidewalk outside, there are many stairways. The entire way, I ruminated about the humiliating conclusion. Opening the door to my car, I heard a voice.

"You can't park there!"

No, it wasn't God. It was my buddy Kyle Cammack joking with me while driving past. But God actually spoke through Kyle's good-natured jab. Kyle had no idea what was happening in my self-absorbed mind. I needed the surprise. It was succinct. It was spot-on. It served. It was a specific answer to prayer that I would later realize was saving me from myself and producing spiritual fruit by pruning. It was creative and smart, coming through the lips of the retired Newport Beach police detective.

Sitting in my car, I realized I had not once consulted God about the Bible study. All those flights of stairs and I'd not had a single thought to pray. Then I was disrupted by, "You can't park there!" I immediately remembered the self-pitying dialogue I'd just read in Jamie Winship's book *Living Fearless*. The book happened to be laying in the passenger seat. I opened right to it. This is what it said:

> Jamie: What do you think about the situation you find yourself in?
>
> Jamie: I'm afraid.

Jamie: I knew it. I'm afraid too.

Jamie: What are you going to do to protect yourself?

Jamie: I was planning on abandoning all hope and running away.

Jamie: Good plan. I'm all in because I think I'm a failure.

Jamie: I agree.

Of course the enemy is willing to chime in.

Enemy: You are right. You are so wise. People aren't paying attention to the facts. They're stupid. You know you're going to lose this thing. When your mother said you were a loser you knew she was right. Wasn't she right?

Jamie: Yeah, she was right.

This lie-based conversation is easy to believe because it never takes faith to believe what's false. Never. But it does take faith to believe what's true. God wants to enter the conversation.

God: You're not in danger. You never are.

Jamie made me laugh. Kyle made me laugh. God made me laugh. The whole ridiculous thing made me laugh. But how could I laugh when I was feeling so raw? It seemed orchestrated that I would see a connection between this event and another discouraging incident, exposing my false identity. I realized that leading a Bible study with Idaho legislators is not who I am; it's what I do for a while. Who I am can never be taken away. What I do will come and go. I will not lead the legislator's Bible study forever. It will go away someday; it's not identity-worthy.

LISTING WHO I AM NOT

A couple of days later, I was sitting in God's presence, reviewing the end of Psalm 139, which we looked at in the senate Bible study. There are six requests in two verses. I wincingly prayed these, inviting God to identify more than the two false selves I was seeking identity from.

"Search me, O God, and know my heart; try me and know my anxious thoughts; and see if there be any hurtful way in me, and lead me in the everlasting way." (Psalm 139:23-24)

In less than an hour, I filled a yellow pad page with a list of 30 pseudo-identities. Fifteen were past things I would skillfully drop into conversations, subtly promoting myself. The problem with false identities is they can be taken away or forgotten, so one constantly needs to keep reminding everyone. Fifteen more were current things, which were not untrue or even necessarily bad things; in fact, they could go on a resume. These things are not who I am in God's eyes—who I am in God's eyes can never be taken away.

So who am I?

I was tasked with writing an identity statement (which I'll share in chapter 10), given by God through Scripture and whispering in my mind's ear.

I now hear God much better, and He surprises me with all He wants to say. Remember that He cannot freely speak to us when we're full of a false sense of self.

> "The most common form of human despair is not being who you are."
>
> — Soren Kierkegaard,
> *The Sickness Unto Death*

ASK. THIS. NOW.

PERSONAL REFLECTION AND GROUP DISCUSSION

Paul attributes the effect of his Gospel-sharing to be a work of the Holy Spirit speaking through him to them, Spirit to spirit, mixing spiritual thoughts with spiritual words. (1 Corinthians 2:16)

What do you think of Dr. Willard's assessment that this is the preferred or more mature way of hearing God's voice? If you embraced this, how would this change the way you hear God?

How would you summarize the difference between these three concepts?

1. The natural man (1 Corinthians 2:14)

2. The spiritual man (1 Corinthians 2:10-13, 15-16)

3. The carnal man (1 Corinthians 3:1-6)

If you read through 1 Corinthians 1-2, you would identify how Paul exposes collective the pseudo-identity present in the Corinthian church, such as pride about their knowledge and wisdom. Jot down any pseudo-identities in your life God may have brought to mind as you read this chapter. Ask Him to expose the false so He can make room for the true.

"Who dwells in God's presence? He who walks with integrity and works righteousness, and speaks truth in his heart." (Psalm 15:1-2)

Appendix: 10-S Answer Key (page 243)

In chapter 8, the 10-S indicators for the Corinthian story were shared. Review them but take a look at how God exposed the false identity in Jon using his senate Bible study story. It will help you think through how a false self is a hindrance to hearing God.

GIVE GOD A MINUTE JOURNAL

You Gotta *Ask*	You Gotta Listen & Watch *Answer*
Date:	

IN THE STILL, SMALL VOICE

> "God only moves where truth is spoken."
> — Jamie Winship

We ended the last chapter saying that God cannot freely speak to us when we're full of false self or falsely full of self. Then again, we need to hear from God to clear out everything false, including false gods, false voices, false identities, and alternate realities. This makes the story in 1 Kings 18-19 helpful on several levels.

Who comes immediately to mind when you think of someone taking on false gods and false prophets? Elijah, of course, taking on the false prophets of Baal. Let's review the epic story.

ELIJAH'S OVERWHELMING VICTORY

In drought-stricken Israel, the prophet Elijah challenged King Ahab and Queen Jezebel to a divine contest on Mount Carmel. Elijah proposed a test to determine the true God: only the real God could send fire to consume a sacrifice.

Ahab's 450 prophets of Baal tried desperately, chanting and even cutting themselves to invoke Baal's favor. However, not a spark came forth. Elijah, in contrast, rebuilt the Lord's altar and soaked his sacrifice in water, showcasing his confidence. After a simple prayer, fire from the heavens consumed Elijah's drenched offering, leaving the crowd in awe.

Witnessing this miracle, the people declared, "The Lord, He is God!" The false prophets were seized, and the people turned back to the Lord. Yet King Ahab and Jezebel were not only unpersuaded, they doubled down, with Jezebel vowing to destroy Elijah's life within 24 hours.

WHAT HAPPENED NEXT?

What perplexes readers is the 180-degree turn Elijah made immediately after. His life was threatened, and he fearfully ran for the hills—alone. He seemed paralyzed with depression and wanted God to take his life. He hid, not eating and sleeping, so God sent an angel to minister to his physical needs and direct him to Mt. Horeb (Sinai), the mountain of God, which was considerably farther away from Jezebel.

The reader wonders, "What happened here? How does this follow such a great spiritual event where God showed up dramatically? God came through exactly how Elijah asked, and even the false prophets were destroyed. How is this not the Super Bowl of religious events?"

But Elijah knew nothing had really changed. The power structures and apostasy in Israel were still in place. He'd shot all of his bullets, and now he was alone. He thought he was as good as dead. He asked God to take his life rather than allow Jezebel to have her way with him. But there was more going on. At the mountain of God, Mt. Horeb/Sinai, where

Moses received the 10 commandments in stone, Elijah had an encounter with God. It sounded like the one the Navy SEAL medic Keith had with God in his dark night: "You're not going to quit, Elijah." Or like He had with Jon: "You can't park there."

The Lord asked him two questions (1 Kings 19:9, 13) and received the *exact same answer* from Elijah both times. (1 Kings 19:10, 14) The first question was in a cave: "What are you doing here, Elijah?"

Elijah's paraphrased answer was "I've been very zealous for You, the warrior God, Who dramatically fought for His people, but they wouldn't keep Your covenant. They tore down Your sacred altars and killed Your prophets, and now they're coming after me. I'm all alone and am as good as dead."

God directed him to go stand on the mountain before the Lord, who was passing by. This sounds exactly like God did with Moses in Exodus 33-34. Same God, same mountain, same pass-by. Then, three dramatic earth-moving events occurred while Elijah stood on the mountain: a great and strong rock-breaking wind, an earthquake, and a fire. After each super phenomena, the text says, "but the Lord was not in it."

God did not come to him in the dramatic—the Earth, Wind, and Fire concert, if you will—but in the small and thin, the sound of gentle silence that followed. A still, small voice or a gentle whisper. (1 Kings 19:11-12)

WHY DOES GOD WHISPER?

C.S. Lewis's *The Screwtape Letters* features a senior demon mentoring his trainee. He makes a brilliant observation. There are two tools God cannot use: He cannot be irresistible, and

He cannot be irrefutable. Why? Because God can easily overwhelm us. And if he does, man will not have the free will to come to Him in genuine love, seeking a relationship. So God comes meekly, kindly, and gently with whispers.

God asked the same question the second time: "What are you doing here, Elijah?" (1 Kings 19:13-14) Elijah gave the same identical answer, explaining that the people were a disaster, the prophets were dead, and he was alone and as good as dead too. It was a true confession of what he believed, but it wasn't where God would let him stay. Thankfully, God is patient and knew a long walk from Mt. Horeb/Sinai through the wilderness to the north of Israel would allow Elijah time to think about the things God revealed along the way.

God explained (my paraphrase), "Elijah, I have three things for you to do. You will anoint two Kings [Hazael over Aram and Jehu over Israel] and a prophet [Elisha] who will continue the fight for Israel's fidelity, each one's effect greater than the previous one. And by the way, there are 7,000 people who have not bowed their knee to Baal. You're not alone." (1 Kings 19:15-21)

"You're not going to quit."

"You can't park there."

THE WHISPER

Have you underestimated the whisper? I have. It illustrates what Paul talks about in 1 Corinthians 2:13: we speak with words taught to us by the Spirit and not with man's wisdom.

Lately, Pam and I have experienced an accelerated movement from God to lift us out of our agnostic narrative to hear His gently whispered message. He wants to speak to us more than we want, or have been able, to hear. His whispers are like a trail of breadcrumbs leading to the bread-maker's bakery. While asking, seeking, and knocking have long been our themes in life and in our co-laboring with God, we've settled for breadcrumbs and not the bakery. We smell the bakery, but we've been timid in asking for more and then being vigilant to hear. His breathy life-giving messages have become breath-taking experiences.

Pam shared two experiences recently that took my breath away. She will finish the chapter by illustrating God's forward-moving, warm, and surprising voice in her spirit, inviting her to move toward Him and be true to who He made her.

PAM'S STORY

Part of hearing God's voice in my life revolves around the discovery of knowing and experiencing God's great love for me. The early draw to give my life to God was hearing that He loves me. Period. I hungered to know I was 100-percent approved and accepted by God. I was searching for this kind of love. In my early teens, I tested the waters and accepted the free gift of this relationship with God—several times, in fact, because I was pretty sure I had blown it and needed to ask again.

As I grew in my understanding that the gift of salvation and love was simply that—free—I began to be more and more in awe of this kind of love. As I have looked back upon my life and asked God in some moments of fear and anxiety, "What am I afraid of?" He finally revealed to me that I was afraid of Him not being there when I really needed Him. I wondered if this could be a fear of abandonment. Yes, it was!

Why would I fear Him not being there for me? It has to do with my early years—years I don't even remember—of not feeling a secure, strong attachment of love. My biological dad died when I was 10 months old in a horrible accident and my mom grieved while doing the best she could to tend to two little girls. She remarried when I was 2, but my new dad was unable to give me the love I needed. My little psyche absorbed this and it impacted me.

Over time, understanding that my true Father *totally* delights in me, loves me deeply, and thinks I'm the bomb has been life-changing! God has been speaking to me and affirming me of His great love for me—not just one time, but continually.

Even despite all the truths that God has spoken over me, I still fall back into my false self and believe lies such as "You aren't enough," "You don't have what it takes," "You are average," or "Others do it better than you." Recently I had yet another breakthrough where God nudged me in that still, small voice.

I was reading *Living Fearless* by Jamie Winship and working through the exercises and practices of asking God what He says about me, like "Who am I?" and "What is my name or what do you call me?" He revealed to me that my name is Love Activist. One of my great joys in life is to help others discover how much God loves them.

Because it has been so transformational for me, I eagerly wanted others to know this. I smiled as I heard God call me an activist since my false self sees me as fearful, ineffective, and average. During COVID, when everyone seemed to be using their loud voices for activism on some front, I felt diminished, quiet, and scared. But God showed me that I have the beautiful ability to come alongside people and help them uncover what is holding them back—often, it's a poor view of how loved they are.

A few months after receiving my name, I was sitting in silence with God and asked Him, "What do you want me to know and do?"

In that still, small voice that Elijah heard, I heard Him say, "Tell me you love me."

What? "Did I hear you right, God?" But I did it, and it totally made sense as to why He would have me do this. I know He loves me, but my hesitancy to say these words is systemic to me believing and receiving His love. You see, I grew up never saying these words—"I love you"—or hearing them. In fact, when Jon told me he loved me for the first time, it took a long time before I could say it back. I knew I loved him but was fearful of declaring it. Declaring my love meant completely trusting and giving myself to him.

Something shifted in me when I told God I loved Him. For me to tell God I love Him involves trust and loving freely and with abandon. I am learning that God is a safe place. He is trustworthy, and His ways are gentle, like the way He speaks to me in that still, small voice.

ASK. THIS. NOW.

PERSONAL REFLECTION AND GROUP DISCUSSION

Have you settled in with the idea illustrated in the Elijah and Pam stories that God speaks to our spirits in a quiet, gentle, affirming, soft way? In contrast, the enemy's voice is loud, screaming, condemning, divisive, and separating.

Assuming you buy in to the "gentle whisper" nature of God's voice, how might this change your listening-to-God habits?

Appendix: 10-S Answer Key (page 244)

The 10-S indicators are on vivid display in chapter 9. The gentle whisper, Spirit to spirit, may be a new paradigm for you and others discussing this book together. At a minimum, review them in the Appendix, but you might want to open up 1 Kings 18-19 and identify them in the context of the story for yourself.

GIVE GOD A MINUTE JOURNAL

You Gotta *Ask*	You Gotta Listen & Watch *Answer*
Date:	

OUR TRUE IDENTITY

"Define yourself radically as one beloved by God. This is the true self. Every other identity is an illusion."
— Brennan Manning

God is whispering to us about our true identities. His whispers expose false identities. Unfortunately, louder voices are drowning out God's voice. In chapter 8, I described how God revealed 30 pseudo-identities I'd glommed onto. They were not bad things per se, but they were things I gained status from that can and will be lost. An identity worth having is anchored in the permanent.

Stripped of the temporary, what is the most fundamental thing about you? What is it grounded in?

WHO WE ARE, FUNDAMENTALLY

My colleague, Don, led an open forum at a recovery facility in southern California. Because Don is a kind, thoughtful, and forthright person, a man approached him with a question following the discussion one day. Don sounded different than most Christians he'd encountered, so he wanted to know what Don thought about his identity as a person on the LGBTQ continuum. Don wisely asked him a thought-provoking question.

"What is the most fundamental thing about you?"

The man pondered this in silence for a moment, then because he didn't have an answer, he asked Don to answer the question for him.

Before I give you Don's answer, how would you answer this question for yourself? Race? Gender? Sexual orientation and preference? Economics? Career? Family bloodline? What?

Don replied, "As a Christ-follower, I believe the most fundamental thing about you and me is we are God's image-bearers and profoundly loved by God as we are." Don's tone of humility and life-giving words were in perfect tandem, connecting with the core longing of this man's soul. The moment was followed by sincere tears.

THE MOST IMPORTANT QUESTION

We all need to answer this question well, but not by ourselves or with a culture that is in an identity free-fall. We need to ask the Creator. When we do, we will find the Creator is also a Redeemer and Restorer of our true humanity.

Recall that I replaced my 30 (or so) pseudo-identities with a succinct, 26-word personal identity statement. It's a mix of Biblical concepts and names God whispered into my mind's ear, Spirit to spirit. A story goes with it, explaining these truths and names. Here is my personal identity statement:

"Created in God's image, I'm a much-loved, chosen, and fully redeemed son, living *true* in the Father, Son, and Spirit's presence as *helper* and *initiator*."

OUR GOD-GIVEN IDENTITIES

The story ignited when Pam's sister, Cindy, asked, "Have you guys heard of Jamie Winship? He sounds a lot like you guys."

Assuming her comment related to Christ-witnessing, we listened to four messages Jamie gave to the Antioch Bible Church youth group. Slowly, we discerned there was much more going on in Jamie and Donna Winship's organization, Identity Exchange. I told Cindy, "Yes, he sounds like us but he is Ph.D. level, and we are third graders hearing God's voice in our identities and our witness."

We were blown away by Jamie's stories of interaction with radical Muslims and all kinds of people internationally and across generations. Muslims were hearing the voice of Jesus through Jamie's in-the-moment introductions, people were hearing from Jesus what He calls them, and more. We began to read Scripture passages about hearing God and how He calls us by name in a new light:

". . . the sheep hear His voice and He calls His own sheep by name and leads them out." (John 10:3)

". . . I have called you by name; you are Mine . . ." (Isaiah 43:1b)

". . . you will be called by a new name which the mouth of the Lord will designate." (Isaiah 62:2b)

"I will give him . . . a new name . . ." (Revelations 2:17c)

We binged on podcast interviews and messages posted on Jamie and Donna's website, IdentityExchange.com. Then we devoured the newly released book *Living Fearless* and took several groups through the book over the next several months. Recently, I participated in a summer intensive online course, Becoming What You Believe. This is where I was prompted to write my personal identity statement.

LOSE THE FAKE IDS

Living Fearless came out of a church men's gathering Jamie led in Salt Lake City. He invited the men (and readers) to lose their "fake IDs" and pray, asking God about their true identities: "How do you refer to us, Lord Jesus?" Then they listened in their mind's ears for the names He calls them.

Just as each sheep had a name given by the shepherd, we can ask God, "What do you call me?"

"God will only call you a name He would call Himself. That's another way you know it's from God. He names us after Himself, like a good father does. He'll call you something that moves you forward in freedom. It's something that excites you, brings you joy and peace. Sometimes what God says about us is almost too beautiful to believe." (Winship, *Living Fearless*, pp. 126-127)

You gotta ask; you gotta listen.

MINDSET CHANGE

Years prior to all this, I took an Enneagram assessment. My profile was number two out of nine possible profiles. It nailed me to the tee, but I hated the title they gave it: "Considerate

Helper." Seriously? Who chose this? All the other numbers get cool names.

Three years passed and when I recently asked God what He calls me, in my mind's ear I heard the word "Helper." What? Wait, that sounds familiar. Did I come up with it? No! I would not come up with this at all. Helper? C'mon.

Jamie also said you might not understand your name. (Many don't initially.) You have to ask God what it means and research it. Allow Him to guide you to fill in the details.

Immediately, God's response to my underwhelmed reaction was, "You know that I call Myself 'Helper,' right? In a dozen Old Testament texts, and most notably Psalm 121:1b-2, 'From whence shall my help come? My help comes from the LORD, who made heaven and earth.'"

Yes, I knew this well. I'd done a word study on the Hebrew word *azer*, translated "help" or "helpmate," some years ago and refreshed on it recently for the senate Bible study in the Psalms.

He continued, "You know Jesus called the Holy Spirit 'the Helper.'" Here, "Helper" is the English translation of the Greek *paraclete*, which means "one called alongside." (John 14, 16)

Yes, I knew this well. Maybe not well enough. Hmmm. Sounded like pseudo-self-residue still hanging around. Researching it more deeply, I've since unearthed some amazing things that fill my soul with enthusiasm and anticipation. The biblical name Ezra is an Aramaic form of the *azer/ezer*. Ezra was a priest who led the restoration of the temple following the Jewish captivity in Babylonia. Jesus was speaking to me about being called a "royal priest" in my study of 1

Peter (2:9). I'm one of the King's priests, interceding and mediating between God and people, inviting them to take the next step toward God.

GOD SPEAKS THE TRUTH

Pam and I have been in full-time vocational ministry all our adult lives. While most people respect this, some people (even close to me) have communicated criticisms of people in this realm who don't have "a real job." Usually, they express it about someone else, but I usually think, "You realize, I too, am that guy. Why are you saying this to me?" When this happens, it feels diminishing. God chose to address this in my heart during an Identity Exchange intensive Zoom call.

In my mind's eye, I was standing in a favorite place, mesmerized by the sparkling Big Spring Creek flowing by my feet. Jesus met me here once when I handed Him a list of false criticisms leveled at me by people in power. He took my list and threw it into the creek, and as it floated away, the ink was blurred to oblivion. There I was again, with Him standing next to me. I was prompted to hand the priestly-calling criticisms to Him. This time He threw the list into the air, not even looking at it. It departed, and instantly a pair of big white wings returned. "Fly in your royal priesthood wings," I heard. That was it.

Prompted to share this with the Zoom group, I described it but felt quite self-conscious. Several others shared amazing images as well.

Then an identity coach, Ray, shared this story about his son, an addict.

INVISIBLE WINGS

Ray's son called him one night, frantic, so Ray calmed him down. "Son, tell me what happened."

"I came out of a bar and grill in the dark after eating dinner. A man yelled at me in the parking lot and said, 'Hey!' He was holding a butcher knife. 'I'm going to do it [kill himself] but I have to talk to you first.'"

Ray told us that his son is a big guy and not afraid to step into a fight. He's also fast. He can fight or he can run and doesn't mind doing either.

His son said, "Dad, I don't know what came over me, but I said, 'Put that knife away. We'll talk.'"

The man put the knife away and said, "I'm a father and grandfather, and look at me." He held his arms out. "I'm a drug addict, and I'm a piece of crap." He then unloaded a diatribe of shame, ending it with, "I'm going to do it." He had decided that he was going to commit suicide with the knife.

To understand what happened next, Ray explained that his son is a functioning alcoholic who knows Jesus but is not a church-going guy.

"God loves you," Ray's son said—out of character for him.

"Yes," the man responded, "because as you walked across the parking lot, a voice told me I needed to talk to you, and when I looked at you, you had wings on."

Ray's son prayed with him, but at the end, the man still responded, "I'm a heroin addict and a piece of crap. God can't love me."

Ray's son confessed, "Sir, I have a drinking problem. I have a potty mouth and talk about people, putting them down when I know I shouldn't. But evidently, God sees me with wings on. And if He sees me with wings on, He sees you with wings on, and you're going to be okay."

Everyone on the Zoom call was rocked by the story. I was double-rocked because what are the odds another story about wings would be told in the same space of 15 minutes on that call? Ray's son, because he is in Christ, is a fellow priesthood holder through no merit of his own—same as me. God put wings on him to be an intercessor and mediator for a man without hope in a dark parking lot. An unlikely evangelist, he invited the man to take a next step toward God.

Indeed, God speaks to and through all kinds of people. Ray's son and I are co-heirs in the grace of life, imperfect but much loved, fully redeemed sons and royal priests with wings. We are not alone in the Kingdom air force, sporting big white wings.

MY IDENTITY

In the days following, God impressed upon me the words *true* and *initiator*. My spiritual gifts—contributions to the body of Christ—come out of this essence, as well as *helper*. I started writing down the names God was giving to many people around me. I marvel at the spot-on creativity of God in naming His sheep. We will share more of these in chapters to follow.

What name might He call you by? You gotta ask; then you gotta listen.

Our culture is in the midst of an identity free fall. People are lost in a sea of chaos, answering the question "Who am I? Who decides? Am I a random accident or special and wanted?" God is willing to answer this question for them if, like Samuel, they are coached to do so.

ASK. THIS. NOW.

PERSONAL REFLECTION AND GROUP DISCUSSION

This application begs to be offered. Simply sit quietly and ask, "Jesus, what do you call me? Speak, Lord, your servant is listening."

What did you hear? If nothing, don't panic. He may answer you very creatively. He is known for customizing responses! Keep watching and listening.

Who can you share this with? Process it. You don't have to understand it right away. Ask God what He wants you to know about what He told you.

Appendix: 10-S Answer Key (page 245)

Ten chapters into the book, you are becoming familiar with the 10-S indicators of hearing God's voice. We've provided the answer key in the Appendix, but you won't be prompted to go look from here on, though the Appendix might be very useful to a group leader in group discussion.

GIVE GOD A MINUTE JOURNAL

You Gotta *Ask*	You Gotta Listen & Watch *Answer*
Date:	

GOD'S WORDS CAN DELIVER US

You gotta listen because God will give His people the words needed and often a way out, delivering us from threatening circumstances. Daniel's three Hebrew colleagues in Babylon come to mind as they stood bright and without compromise before the tyrannical edict of King Nebuchadnezzar and the threat of his fiery furnace. The story is told in Daniel 3.

ROYAL PRIESTS

Peter calls the followers of Christ in Asia Minor (modern-day Turkey) "royal priests." (1 Peter 1:2; 2:9) The eternal Kingdom—the new heaven on the new earth—will be our permanent dwelling. In the meantime, we Christ-followers are intercessors and mediators between God and all kinds of people. We are a Kingdom of priests. *All* of us.

A small percentage of us, like Pam and I, carry out vocational ministry callings, but all Christ-followers, whatever their vocation or occupation, are given authority from heaven to make disciples of Jesus on earth, with Jesus always present. (Matthew 28:18-20) We are to put on our wings and fly in

God's sovereign calling and placement, each having access to people through networks of family, work, recreation, and neighborhoods. As I have mentioned before, in these places, we will find what Jesus called "the other sheep who will hear My voice too."

GOD TERRAIN VEHICLES

The next two chapters will feature God speaking to and through His royal priestly mediators in "real world" vocations. God dwells in us through the Holy Spirit, and we are what I like to call GTVs—God terrain vehicles, moving throughout the planet. As roving temples of the Holy Spirit, people sense the God-*aroma* (2 Corinthians 2:14-17) in us, but they don't always understand that it is God and may not value what we possess. (1 Corinthians 2:12-16) Watching us live creates tension in them, for they are both attracted to and repelled by us. Those hearing His voice might be in either state at any given time. Mostly, we will mystify them.

The Holy Spirit residing in us, speaking to us, and bearing fruit through us as we live under His influence evokes reactions. Abiding in Jesus, hearing and obeying His voice, evokes reactions. In unplanned circumstances, such as the story to follow, we may be put on the spot in frightening circumstances and not know what will come out of our mouths. Jesus said He would give us the words, and He is true to His word.

Sometimes, Jesus prompts us to prepare and gives us wise words ahead of time. (1 Peter 3:15) This is featured in the next chapter. Most of us prefer this method, but sometimes we simply cannot anticipate what we will step into. I may be one of the most prepared people because of formal and practiced training. Yet I still fear I won't know what to say or I won't say it well enough. Jesus knows this about us. It's why He gave this promise to us when he spoke these words to his disciples:

". . . do not worry beforehand about what you are to say, but say whatever is given you in that hour; for it is not you who speak, but it is the Holy Spirit." (Mark 13:11)

THE RIGHT WORDS AT THE RIGHT TIME

I love my friend Kent Bader and the following story. I tell it all the time. In fact, I now know the story better than Kent and have to correct him on details sometimes.

> A number of years ago, I [Kent] was assigned as lead discipline engineer on an Intel design project in Portland. This was my first project as lead engineer and it required work on-site in Portland throughout the design phase. So every weekday and every other weekend, I was in Portland without my family. On any project, one of my objectives was to get to know my clients on a personal level. Going beyond the client-consultant relationship into a personal friendship has always had many positive benefits, including less tension, more grace, more fun, and opportunities to share my faith.
>
> The difficulty is often that the client is very worldly, raising the question of how far I am willing to go with them into their world. Jon Strain said to me, "I go as far into the culture as I can, right up to but not past the point of sin." He articulately expressed what I felt should be the case. This seemed to best line up with what Paul was talking about in 1 Corinthians 9:22: "I have become all things to all men, so that I might by all means save some."
>
> On this project in Portland, my Intel client was named Mike. He was a fairly recent graduate and also newly married.

Despite differences in age, moral values, and worldview, we got to be good friends. We got together for breakfast or lunch four or five times a week, and he and his wife would have me over for dinner once every other week or so. Our friendship was pretty uncommon. One Friday night, Mike invited me to a party with the guest list consisting almost entirely of Intel folks and their spouses. Honored to be included, I had a great time getting to know a number of them outside of our work project. My "test" came late that evening.

Mike suggested that everyone go to a strip joint. This idea gained momentum with the entire group as they began chanting, "Strip club, strip club!" There was no way I was going, and I planned to just leave—no fuss, no muss. Then Mike asked me directly if I was going with them. I told him quietly that I was tired and would be going back to my hotel room to go to bed, a nice, low-risk response. His wife overheard me and piped up in a loud, shrill voice, "Oh no, you're not! You're going with us."

Immediately, I was the sole focus of attention and everyone was clamoring for me to go, chanting, "Kent, Kent, Kent!" At that moment, I felt more peer pressure than I had ever experienced in my life. A number of things raced through my mind. First, it was neat to realize how much a part of that group I had become. I was one of them, a membership with many advantages both personally and professionally. But, by rejecting their offer, I may end up souring a number of valued relationships, my newfound status in the group, and damaging my career. I would be lying if I said that I wasn't afraid. But was it worth dishonoring my God, my wife, my daughters, and myself? No. And in the end, who should I really fear?

That night the Holy Spirit put the perfect words in my mouth. In a voice that everyone could hear, I said, "If I'm going to spend money on a woman, it's going to be on my wife, who is my best friend, or my precious daughters. Good night!"

With that, I left. On my way back to the hotel, I assumed that I had blown a number of relationships. On Monday, I learned it was exactly the opposite. No one went to the strip joint. Everyone simply left to go home after my departure. Instead of losing people's respect, I actually gained ground.

This was evident a few evenings later when Mike and I, with another Intel employee not at the party, went out for dinner. The other man suggested we all buy a round of tequila shots. I told him pleasantly that I only drank in moderation and that I didn't want to drink shots. He responded fairly harshly and, in no uncertain terms, asserted I would be drinking shots or that he, the client, would be unhappy. Mike exploded on him, saying, "Kent doesn't compromise on his values, and you better back off!"

Kent Bader, God terrain vehicle (GTV) on the road at work, told me later he had no idea what he was going to say when he opened his mouth. He was transcended as Jesus gave him the words—beautiful, bar-lifting, true words, custom-fit for the listeners. Plus, they had a surprising effect in the moment, the next day, and even days later. Perhaps those words still live on in some way with the original hearers. They certainly live on for *us* to read and ponder, perhaps so we too can trust Jesus to give us the words when needed.

"Those who have insight will shine brightly like the brightness of the expanse of heaven, and those who lead the many to righteousness, like the stars forever and ever." (Daniel 12:3)

ASK. THIS. NOW.

PERSONAL REFLECTION AND GROUP DISCUSSION

Have you had an experience like Kent's where you and your faith convictions were put on the spot? Maybe you even heard God say something to you or through you. How did it work out?

You've read several examples of people on the hotseat, such as Ananias and Daniel's three friends Shadrach, Meshach, and Abednego. How does Jesus speak to our fear in witnessing? (Mark 13:11) And why does Jesus tell us not to worry? (Mark 13:10)

"... say whatever is given you in that hour, for it is not you who speak, but it is the Holy Spirit." —Jesus, to his disciples (Mark 13:11)

Appendix: 10-S Answer Key (page 246)

If you're leading a group discussion, use the chapter 11 section of the Appendix for the Scripture passages reinforcing Daniel 3.

You can also have some fun analyzing how many 10-S characteristics are in Kent's story.

GIVE GOD A MINUTE JOURNAL

You Gotta *Ask*	You Gotta Listen & Watch *Answer*
Date:	

PREPARING FOR THE MOMENT

Like Kent Bader when confronted with a less-than-comfortable situation like the one told in the previous chapter, we can always be prayerful and watchful in all circumstances. We trust God will give us the words in situations we couldn't possibly prepare specific words for. We answer out of our lives—our values, commitments, and decisions made ahead of time. If you know how to listen, when under pressure, "say whatever is given you in that hour, for it is not you who speak, but the Holy Spirit." (Mark 10:13)

LIVING A LIFE OF READINESS

We should always be in training. God gives us words in the moment, but we need to live a lifestyle of readiness to engage. This readiness is found in the framework of 1 Peter 3:15 and its context:

". . . but sanctify Christ as Lord in your hearts, always being ready to make a defense to everyone who asks you to give an account for the hope that is in you, yet with gentleness and reverence . . ."

THE THREE TYPES OF PREPAREDNESS

Let's look at the three parts of this one Scripture:

1. SPIRITUALLY PREPARED

King Jesus is one and only.

"... but sanctify Christ as Lord in your hearts ..." (1 Peter 3:15a)

"Sanctify" means to set apart as holy. Holy means unique, like no other. Christ the Messiah is the eternal King of Daniel 7:13-14. King Jesus is our ultimate. We give Him the ultimate place in our hearts, relationships, lives, and everything we have. (Luke 14:25-35) He is a conquering King but seeks to win our hearts through kindness. He is the commander who lays down His life for His soldiers and the Shepherd who leaves the 99 and goes after the once lost sheep. He is the ultimate voice because He is seated on the throne.

He is the king and ground commander in the mission to share His story. We have authority from Heaven and a leader who knows everything about the situation coordinating a massive multi-level and complex mission. We are not alone. (Matt 28:18-20) Remember that we are God terrain vehicles, moving about the Earth, hardwired for guidance and companionship with software to give and receive messages in real time.

2. INTELLECTUALLY PREPARED

The Gospel of King Jesus is the only hope.

"... always being ready to make a defense to everyone who asks you to give an account for the hope that is in you ..." (1 Peter 3:15b)

The Gospel is the good news of His history-changing victory over sin and death. The defense is reasoned and verbal, such as one might hear in a courtroom. It contains eyewitness testimonies, exhibits, and forensic evidence of something that happened in history. We need to become adept at describing the change that Jesus has brought to our lives, offering hope to those who have none. Aside from Jesus, no one has answered the problem of death, sin, and suffering.

3. SOCIALLY PREPARED

Messengers of amazing grace should be gracious.

". . . yet with gentleness and reverence . . ." (1 Peter 3:15c)

Instead of exchanging bullets for bullets, we exchange blessings for whatever comes at us. We have nothing to fear or anyone to be intimidated by because even if the worst should happen and we die, we will ultimately be with Jesus in Heaven. We can suffer for what is right because we know the people doing the wrongs only have temporary power. We are blessed people eternally, so we give eternal blessings. All hardship is temporary, and at the end, we will be with Jesus. (1 Peter 2:21-25; 3:8-18; 4:12-4, 19; 5:11-12)

OUR TRUE ENEMY

People are not the enemy. People are POWs. They are looking for something or someone to spring them from the difficulties of planet Earth—evil, suffering, and death—but have developed a spiritual Stockholm syndrome when hostages or abuse victims bond with their captors or abusers over time.

What else do they have? As the disciples asked Jesus, "To whom shall we go? You have the words of eternal life." (John

6:68) Ask yourself, who else has the words of eternal life with any credibility? I am well aware of historical, philosophical, and religious leaders, and no one holds a candle to Jesus. In Him alone is hope.

"Our struggle is not against flesh and blood, but against the rulers, against the powers, against the world forces of this darkness, against the spiritual forces of wickedness in the heavenly places." (Ephesians 6:12)

Paul tells the entire unit, the body of Christ, God's terrain vehicles, to put on the full armor of God and move forward together as a unit—picture the Roman tortoise with shields overhead and on the sides. Standing firm together, he explains the three-way conversation—God to us, us to God, us to POWs, and POWs to God, all moving to reconciling people to God.

"With all prayer and petition pray at all times in the Spirit [who indwells each of us and all of us], and with this in view, be on the alert with all perseverance and petition for all the saints, [19] and pray on my behalf, that utterance may be given to me in the opening of my mouth, to make known with boldness the mystery of the Gospel, [20] for which I am an ambassador in chains; that in proclaiming it I may speak boldly as I ought to speak." (Ephesians 6:18-20)

Christ-soldiers and ambassadors with military comms headsets, or rather, inner earpieces, listen to the direction and commands of King Jesus through the Holy Spirit. God is speaking to the captives who have glommed onto their captors in fear. We are inviting them to be free and join God's side and to make our conquering and compassionate King their king too. We explain the terms of a pardon offered (the Gospel of grace), inviting them to speak with our King-Commander to make it official. Jesus is speaking to and through all kinds of people. These are the *other sheep* whom He says will hear His voice. (John 10:16)

In summary, these are the 1 Peter 3:15 essentials:

1. Listen to and obey your commander in real time.
2. Engage as a team and perform your role according to your training.
3. Never forget who—and whose—you are and how, through tone and ethics, He wants you to engage.

A HEART-OPENING QUESTION TO A DIRECT CHALLENGE

Scott Greco provides a beautiful example of listening, tactics, and tone recorded below. He served a 20-year adventure in the U.S. Army, primarily as an attack helicopter pilot. In between combat tours, he discovered his love for teaching when he served as an instructor at West Point, his alma mater, and as a professor of military science at the University of Tampa. Scott knows the importance of preparation and planning for both a combat mission and teaching a course. You prepare well because you don't always know what's going to be thrown at you. Much of the time, you are ready, but there are times you couldn't possibly anticipate a situation. You have to trust that your training—predetermined choices, practices, and commitments—will kick in.

A few days ago, an acquaintance approached me and asked me what I thought of the recent SCOTUS opinion regarding abortion. I knew that he had some assumptions about my thoughts and that he was ready for a spirited debate that I really did not want to engage in. For days, I had been reading or hearing comments filled with frustration, disappointment, sadness, anger, and even rage, and I did not want to add to that fire.

I asked if I could first ask him a question, and he kindly agreed. I then asked him, "What is the single most important thing in the world to you?"

He smiled, stated that he wasn't sure, that it would take him a while to think about the answer, and that he wanted to hear my answer. I said that it was Jesus and my relationship with him. I then said that the reason I asked him that question was because my answer to that question shapes everything about how I would answer his original SCOTUS question and that I wondered if he would be in a similar situation. He followed with an, "Okay, gotcha." The conversation essentially stopped there.

My hope is that I will be able to get his answer to my question soon, and that I'll be able to continue to avoid an unproductive discussion about the Supreme Court. Much of our nation is unhinged right now, and Jesus is the Rock that they need. I may be accused of dodging the question, but I think we can use this opportunity to talk about the most important thing with our family, friends, colleagues, and neighbors who are searching for something firm to grab hold of.

THE IMPORTANCE OF KNOWING WHO WE ARE

Like Kent Bader in the last chapter, Scott Greco lives in awareness of his identity as a chosen, much loved, and fully redeemed follower of Christ. Like Kent, he is aware of his intercessory and mediator role between God and people in any setting, including work. Like Kent, he wants "to proclaim the excellencies of Him who has called you out of darkness into His marvelous light." (1 Peter 2:9)

Both men are vigilant to Peter's command, "Keep your behavior excellent among the Gentiles [people without God] so that in the thing in which they slander you as evildoers, they may because of your good deeds, as they observe them, glorify God in the day of visitation." (1 Peter 2:12)

Scott's question, "What is the single most important thing in the world to you?" is gently exposing and laced with qualities rooted in 1 Peter 3:15. It disarmed the land mine of a potentially explosive and polarizing question, keeping the Gospel of King Jesus the main thing. Scott's question and brief explanation were sincere. He invited reflection of what was of ultimate importance to the man. It kept the door open. It was appropriate in the workspace.

PREPARING FOR NEXT TIME

This encounter was brilliantly formed ahead of time by Scott's interaction with the Holy Spirit about a premonition of such a question coming his way. After the confrontation, Scott had time to prepare thoughts on what Jesus and His word say about abortion.

Scott has a band of brothers to meet and explore this with, which includes me. Together, we learned from Scott's model of a great question and thought through a Jesus response. Specifically, we discussed what Scott could, would, or should say to answer the question of abortion. To engage them, I brought a trifold brochure titled "Everything Jesus Said About Abortion." Opening the brochure, it was completely *empty*. Jesus said nothing specifically. Yet Scripture says much about the identities of babies inside and outside the womb—even pre-conception! We filled the brochure in together and prepared to give an account of the hope within us and to share the truth graciously.

Among many, abortion is a hot-button issue to navigate well. The next chapter will address why it is critical we do so, all the while keeping the focus on the most important thing— the Gospel of amazing grace, full of grace and truth. We will go inside the world of POWs, where hearing the voice of Jesus in real time is critical.

ASK. THIS. NOW.

PERSONAL REFLECTION AND GROUP DISCUSSION

Was there something in this chapter you were attracted to or challenged by?

What do the four points of readiness in 1 Peter 3:15 contribute to your understanding of witnessing for Jesus?

How does 1 Peter 3:15a, "but sanctify Christ as Lord in your hearts," connect with the instruction of Jesus in Mark 13:11, ". . . say whatever is given you in that hour; for it is not you who speak, but it is the Holy Spirit"? How does Scott Greco's story model both statements?

Appendix: 10-S Answer Key (page 247)

Chapter 12's 10-S indicators of God's voice will enhance your answers to the Personal Reflection and Group Discussion questions.

GIVE GOD A MINUTE JOURNAL

You Gotta *Ask*	You Gotta Listen & Watch *Answer*
Date:	

JESUS, THE HEALER AND LIBERATOR

"Three things keep us from hearing the voice of God: unforgiveness, anger, and self-hatred."
— Jamie Winship, Identity Exchange Summer Intensive

Is there any front more volatile, in the public square and in the soul, than abortion? Yet, even here, Jesus is speaking to and through all kinds of people. Jesus, the healer and liberator, comes on the scene of brokenness and creates beauty. You will see this in the text that launched Jesus's public ministry embedded between two illustrating modern stories: the inventor of modern-day search and rescue and the Rachel's Vineyard post-abortion retreat.

THE POWER OF THE VOICE OF JESUS

These stories show us that when we see into the inner worlds of others, it changes us. When broken people hear the voice of Jesus through us, it changes them. To get there, you gotta ask and you gotta listen, both person to person and to God about the person. In the battle zone, we enter to fight for people, but we don't fight them. We enter without judgment because they are already judged, stuck in ravines of guilt, overwhelmed by mountain-sized fear, and carried away by rivers of molten-lava anger. That's a bit dramatic, but it sets up what kind of help they need—nonjudgmental search and rescue. This is when and where they hear His voice.

STORY 1: SEARCH AND RESCUE WITHOUT JUDGEMENT

Minor Harkness is the inventor of modern-day search and rescue. By modern day, I mean he introduced hound dogs and helicopters to rescues, among other things. I shared breakfast with him in Sun Valley, Idaho, to hear the story. He carried his "rescue notebooks" into the diner, an aged man with a serious limp—not from risky rescues, but from a Moped scooter accident on vacation. His notebooks contained newspaper clippings of rescues that guided our discussion.

Minor was an insurance man living in the greater Los Angeles area. He observed many people getting into trouble in the Sierra Madre mountains but knew there were very few people to rescue them with wisdom, skill, and timeliness. Surprisingly, most search and rescue was, and still is, volunteer-based. His insurance business afforded him the flexibility to be a lead volunteer rescuer.

When he learned about the search and rescue code, he got a big surprise. "Search and rescue is not judgmental. We simply go get them whether they deserve it or not." This was foundational in the written search and rescue code. Minor said, "Law enforcement is judgmental and will write you tickets for harmful and foolish choices. Believe me, there are many who didn't deserve help because they were doing drugs or engaging in foolish behavior."

JESUS'S MISSION TO SEEK AND SAVE

Search and rescue is not judgmental. The parallels with Jesus and His rescue mission, announced at the beginning of His public ministry in Luke 4:16-21, are striking. In Luke 15, Jesus responded to the judgmental Pharisees soured by His dining with tax collectors and sinners. (Luke 15:1-2) Jesus responded by telling three consecutive parables about the lost sheep, the lost coin, and the two lost sons, all making the same point: Jesus came to seek and save the lost ones. By "lost," He meant missing and valuable. At the home of the chief tax collector, Zaccheus, Jesus summarized his mission: "For the Son of Man has come to seek and to save that which was lost." (Luke 19:10)

In the Nazareth synagogue, Jesus was handed the Isaiah scroll to read, which providentially contained the text He used to announce His public ministry. He turned to what we know as Isaiah 61:1 and read what is recorded in Luke 4:18-19:

> *The Spirit of the Lord upon Me,*
> *Because LORD has anointed Me to preach the gospel to the poor.*
> *He has sent Me to proclaim release to the captives,*
> *And recovery of sight to the blind,*
> *To set free those who are oppressed,*
> *To proclaim the favorable year of the Lord.*

Then Jesus added, "Today this Scripture has been fulfilled in your hearing." (Luke 4:21)

Unfortunately, the synagogue was filled with law-enforcement people, and things escalated with them acting as prosecutors who tried to throw Him down the brow of a hill, although He escaped. (4:22-30)

For the already condemned, judgment is not helpful. Following the familiar verse of John 3:16 is John 3:17, "For God did not send the Son into the world to judge the world, but that the world should be saved through Him."

So if we Christ-followers are search and rescue and not law enforcement, why all the judging, condemning, canceling, separating, and isolating? Aren't we chasing people off instead of moving toward the captive, the blind, and the downtrodden—whether it is their fault or not?

STORY 2: HEALING AT RACHEL'S VINEYARD

No issue burns more hotly than abortion. Yes, we are trying to save babies' lives. And millions are suffering from their participation in abortion. There is no part of a woman's life not affected by abortion. I've witnessed this firsthand for years.

Rachel's Vineyard hosts a weekend retreat for men and women whose lives have been impacted by abortion. The ministry is year-round, yet features the most powerful retreat experience I've ever witnessed or participated in. For 16 years, I've participated as a Protestant pastor amidst a Roman Catholic Church-sponsored ministry. Non-Catholics participate, too, and that's why I'm included. Whatever there is to "protest" between Protestants and Roman Catholics is laid to rest for a weekend like this. I have nothing to protest about what happens during the weekend.

My colleagues are a priest or two, a deacon, a therapist or two, and the real heroes, an amazing team of women who make the weekend possible with their undying labor of love year-round. Plus, there are scores of prayer warriors, both on- and off-site, praying before, during, and after this powerful healing time. It is intense and taxing. It's hard to count how many others quietly serve in practical matters of hospitality. I don't think I exaggerate when I say the ratio of hosts to retreatants must be 5:1.

From dinner on Friday to the Sunday afternoon memorial service where named and grieved-for children are surrendered to God, we witness miracle upon miracle of multi-level healing. Officiating the memorial service each year, I read Luke 4:21-26, "Today this Scripture has been fulfilled in your hearing." Then I add the word "again." Again and again, every year Jesus shows up to speak and perform healing and liberation among the most devastated people I've ever met.

The brokenness among the participants is painfully evident Friday evening when retreatants arrive and are sitting in a circle. They are stressed, downcast, sometimes medicated, and appear ready to bolt from the facility. The first miracle is their arrival. It's fragile. It's a battle. But they are loved head to toe, breath to breath, moment to moment, exercise to exercise, and a.m. to p.m. They experience the utmost in care, prayer, hospitality, listening, and timely guidance.

Jesus begins to speak to them and to us about them. Here's how: We listen all weekend, which can be difficult for a guy like me who likes to move. I estimate 95 percent of our participation is listening. It took me three years to fully realize how important this was to the women retreatants who have had very poor experiences with men in their lives. A major part of their healing is loving men listening and sharing in their suffering. And praying. And masculine humor at the right moments. It sounds odd, but there is much humor experienced during the weekend, though not on Friday evening.

Aside from the abortions, there is profound brokenness on all life fronts. Consequently, they experience bondage to the three things that keep anyone from hearing the voice of God: unforgiveness, anger—sometimes rage—and self-hatred. The demons are many, the voices are confusing, the condemnation is relentless and pounding. These voices mix with those of past abusers and neglectors, fueling their own self-talk and narratives and imprisoning them with fear, shame, and guilt. They are invited to carry a weighty rock of burden (collected on Friday night) until they are ready to surrender it sometime during the weekend, when they will exchange it for a blessing.

In various breathtaking ways, they begin to hear and experience the voice of the Good Shepherd, who gently moves into their toxic lockboxes of memory. Jesus shushes all other voices through loving hospitality, a variety of living Scripture readings and reflections, and prayers of blessing, confession, and invitation. They tell their abortion stories and the things contributing to it. It is often the first time most of them hear another person's story. They participate in guided therapeutic role-playing and various tactile exercises. There is a lot of opportunity for them to mix with hosts and fellow retreatants, who become a major part of their healing process. They begin to stand with each other in the battle. Jesus speaks to and through all kinds of people, much like the Samaritan woman who became the evangelist to her city.

Micro and macro breakthroughs happen throughout the weekend. Saturday afternoon's therapeutic role-playing session is when it's quite noticeable. It was heart-pounding for me the first few years when I would be invited to be the stand-in man—boyfriend, husband, father, etc.—when a woman read her letter to one who used, abused, and/or abandoned her. The Spirit of Jesus gave me premonitions that I would be called on. And He gave me wisdom, insight, or a slant to take about how I was to respond. I regularly experienced "I will give you the words."

One year, I was invited to hear Cathleen's letter. I had a clear message in my inner ear: "Be ready for anything; take whatever comes to you." *Was I going to get slugged in the face?* I wondered as I pulled my chair over to face hers. Cathleen read her letter, then nervously rolled it up like a newspaper while elaborating about her rage toward the person she wrote to and whom I was representing. Then she whacked me on the head with the rolled-up letter. I'm not kidding. It didn't hurt at all, but everyone in the room gasped. As instructed by the Holy Spirit, I took it and didn't break eye contact.

She then invited me to respond to her letter. I don't know how the man who deserved to be whacked would have responded, but I was led to respond as a regretful, later-in-life, mature man who had years to reflect. I told her, "I think about it a lot. I'm deeply sorry. I didn't know what to do. Will you forgive me?"

The therapist guided her to work through her anger, finding and giving forgiveness. Other participants stood with her, empowering her response. Then we ended in a big hug.

Guess what? Cathleen is a professional therapist, and she has become one of the therapist guides for the retreat. She was even the main facilitator one year. Unbelievable. We have a great story to tell and laugh about it every year. Great news, healing, liberation, and release visit us because Jesus speaks to and through all kinds of people, even a roomful of people whose lives have been tragically impacted by abortion.

> "Abortion denies the unborn of a valuable future."
> — Don Marquis, atheist philosopher and professor

People know deep down what Professor Marquis means. But judgment doesn't deliver people from their hurt and fear. The voice of Jesus, full of grace and truth, experienced in and through His people, delivers.

THOSE WHO NEED JESUS

Reconsider the Isaiah 61:1 themes that define Jesus as the healing liberator of POWs:

> The *afflicted*: the poor, humble, and needy hear the good news announced in the face of death.

> The *broken-hearted*: Jesus binds up and heals the broken, fragmented pieces because abortion impacts every part of a person's being: physical, emotional, spiritual, and relational for life.

> The *captives*: Jesus liberates them to run free, having been POWs due to the choices of others. People in power deprived them of their voice, good conscience, and will to choose.

> The *prisoners*: bound by real guilt, prison doors open because they're pardoned and freed.

NEW LIFE

You can see it in their faces on Sunday morning, a stark contrast with Friday night. It looks like a completely different group of people. There is joy and light-heartedness. They feel safe, united, affirmed, and loved. One year, a woman expressed reluctance about leaving and returning to "the real world." Deacon Chuck Skoro classically replied, "*This* is the real world!" It's the real world as God intends it to be, and we can live in His presence and resources forever.

REPRESENTING JESUS

In much of the retreat, the voice of God is heard in weeping and groaning. During the living Scripture reading of Jesus raising Lazarus from the dead (John 11), we role-play a portion of the script, including "Jesus wept." Father Crowley wailed loudly the first year I participated. When he didn't return, I was asked to fill the weeping Jesus role. Not a chance. I'm no Hollywood actor. Mostly, it's just a little too vulnerable. It felt like they asked me to do it every year. And up until recently, my answer was always a resounding no.

Two years ago, God prepared me for a yes when I was studying Romans 8 where it describes three groaners amidst the suffering of planet Earth: The Holy Spirit groans, we groan, and the Earth groans. (8:22-23, 26) God spoke to me: "Instead of a weeping wailer, what if you could be a groaning, sighing weeper?" I already do this a lot as planet Earth, and it's suffering wears me out. So I was the first groaning weeper Jesus at the Boise Rachel's Vineyard retreat. Apparently, it was acceptable, since I was asked again.

Using poetic license, here's Mark 10:13: "I will give you the words, the ears, the tears, and the groans. So don't worry about it. Show up for others, and you'll receive what you need when you need it."

ASK. THIS. NOW.

PERSONAL REFLECTION AND GROUP DISCUSSION

Was there something in this chapter you were attracted to or challenged by?

How do 1 Peter 3:15a, ". . . but sanctify Christ as Lord in your hearts, always being ready . . ." and the instruction of Jesus in Mark 13:11, ". . . say whatever is given you in that hour; for it is not you who speak, but it is the Holy Spirit," coincide in the way God spoke through Jon and the team at the Rachel's Vineyard retreat?

What is God whispering to you right now? If it's quiet, what is the last thing you recall God saying to you? Invite God to speak: "Father, Son, and Holy Spirit, what do you want me to know? What do you want me to do?"

Appendix: 10-S Answer Key (page 248)

Chapter 13's 10-S indicators of God's voice will enhance your answers to the Personal Reflection and Group Discussion questions.

GIVE GOD A MINUTE JOURNAL

You Gotta *Ask*	You Gotta Listen & Watch *Answer*
Date:	

OUR IDENTITY FROM CONCEPTION

We come out of the birth canal into a battle zone. For millions, the battle zone begins in the fallopian tube, where sperm and egg form a zygote. Warring voices are in open conflict about what the zygote is exactly. Is it human? When does it become human? Does it have a human identity? Who decides? If the zygote, turned blastocyst, turned embryo, turned fetus, makes it out of the womb to be called a baby, that baby will remain under assault about his or her identity and value for the rest of its life. The shelling doesn't cease until death, and sometimes beyond.

CHILDREN CAN HEAR HIS VOICE

In the midst of the warfare of voices and choices, Jesus speaks to and through all kinds of people all their lives. He speaks to children like Samuel, who could not recognize His voice until taught. (1 Samuel 3) Most of the time, they are not taught until they are adults, if ever. The angel Gabriel declared that, in the womb, John would be filled with the Holy Spirit. At six months' gestation, when Jesus entered the womb of Mary, John did a reverse somersault. ". . . the baby leaped in her womb; and Elizabeth was filled with the Holy Spirit . . ." Then Elizabeth added, ". . . the baby leaped in my womb for joy." (Luke 1:41, 44) How did the fetus, already named John by God, know? The Holy Spirit was present in both babies in the wombs.

We can see that John's and Jesus's identities and callings were first created in the mind of God, then formed in the wombs of Elizabeth and Mary pre-birth. What do we, and each child, need to know about our God-gifted identity? Like John and Jesus, identity and purpose started in the creative, loving joint mind of the Father, Son, and Holy Spirit before the foundation of the world. (Ephesians 2:10)

IS IT SOMETHING OR SOMEBODY IN THE WOMB?

Luke answers this question with undisputed clarity. In three chapters (Luke 1, 2, and 18), his unique usage of the Greek word *brephos*, applies to both pre-born and newborn children, starting with John the Baptist and Jesus. This specific word usage is weighty in terms of God-given identity and purpose, which are defined *before* conception. (Luke 1:41, 44; 2:12, 16) The more common word for children, *paidion*, is used from newborn to maturing children. This was the word Matthew used in the birth story of Jesus. Only Luke employs *brephos*. (It's no surprise as he uniquely uses other medical terminology in Luke and Acts.) He is more precise than the tax collector, Matthew. Both terms are employed when quoting Jesus in Luke 18. Jesus's teaching is significant because there is nothing essentially different between a preborn and a newborn. Only maturity.

"And they were bringing even their babies [*brephos*] to Him so that He would touch them, but when the disciples saw it, they began rebuking them. [16] But Jesus called for them, saying, 'Permit the children [*paidion*] to come to Me, and do not hinder them, for the kingdom of God belongs to such as these. [17] Truly I say to you, whoever does not receive the kingdom of God like a child [*paidion*] will not enter it at all.'" (Luke 18:15-17)

The voice of Jesus through Luke matters. Children are fully human, starting in the mind of God at conception, at every stage of development in the womb, and after birth into adulthood. How will the children hear the voice of Jesus if they're not permitted to draw near? Why are we allowing stumbling blocks to hearing His voice and finding their identity in His image? And it's serious if you read Matthew 18:1-10. "See to it that you do not despise one of these little ones, for I say to you that their angels in heaven continually see the face of My Father who is in heaven." (Matthew 18:10)

THE NEW EVANGELISM

Here's a question Steve Petermeyer, an identity coach with Jamie Winship, asked a gathering at our home: "What if every believer *learned* to hear God?" (What if this included children, like Samuel in 1 Samuel 3?) Steve continued, "It's not for believers only, for *everyone* can hear the voice of God all their lives." Steve refers to this as "the new evangelism." It's actually the oldest evangelism in the world because God has been speaking to all kinds of people throughout history, starting with Adam in the garden, who had two-way, real-time conversations with God. Abraham, hearing God's voice, knew enough to believe the far-reaching covenant God made with him. (Genesis 12, 15) He had no Bible, but this covenant became the basis of our 66-book Bible. Moses spoke with God in conversation as two friends. Moses had no Bible, yet his conversations with God became the first five books (the Torah) of our Bible. Consider other youths, besides Samuel—King Josiah, David, Daniel, Shadrach, Meshach, and Abednego—who heard God's voice. Mary, Jesus's young teen mother, heard God's voice.

MARY'S RESPONSE TO GOD'S MESSAGE

Contrast how well Mary heard and received God's voice compared to advanced-in-years professional priest Zacharias—the father of John the Baptist. Both pregnancy announcements could have been solid cases for modern-day abortions. Mary's could be labeled an unwanted pregnancy because she was not fully wed to Joseph yet. The appearance of scandal was real as she was pregnant by someone other than her betrothed, Joseph. Elizabeth was advanced in years and too old to bear children, therefore a high-risk pregnancy. God knew their wombs nurtured great people.

Mary was betrothed (legally married, but not consummated) when the angel Gabriel announced, "And behold, you will conceive in your womb and bear a son, and you shall name Him Jesus. He will be great and be called the Son of the Most High; and the Lord God will give Him the throne of His father David and He will reign over the house of Jacob forever, and His kingdom will have no end." Luke 1:31-33

Note that Jesus is named, anointed, called, and identified as the eternal King *before* He is conceived as a zygote. This is a God-given identity with a corresponding purpose, all announced pre-conception.

Mary said many marvelous things in response, but what she said first is most important. "Behold, the bondslave of the Lord; may it be done to me according to your word." (Luke 1:38) Paraphrased: "Bring it."

ZACHARIAS'S RESPONSE TO GOD'S MESSAGE

Contrast Zacharias's response to the pregnancy announcement brought by Gabriel. He's more like the rest of us. A wee bit agnostic, "How will I know this for certain?" (Luke 1:18b) You judge if this is an appropriate response to everything Gabriel presents as Zacharias serves in the Holy of Holies, fulfilling a once-in-a-lifetime service. Like Mary, "fear gripped him" when he saw the angel, and both are told not to fear for there is great news. (Luke 1:12-13, 28-30) Then the angel announces John the Baptist's identity, role, and birth.

Note that John's name, identity, calling, consecration, anointing, and announcement of fulfilled prophecy (Malachi 4:6) is all *pre-conception* (Luke 1:24). Zacharias's long-standing prayer request is being answered. Gabriel announces it is great news to rejoice over.

Allow me to be a little snarky on behalf of Gabriel to the underwhelming response of Zacharias.

"Zach! Why do you need to *know for certain*? We didn't need to tell you. It's a courtesy call—a heads-up. What difference will it make for you to know for certain? Either she's going to have the baby or not. It's not on you; your part is easy. Plus, this is the answer to your multiple requests for a child. You've worn us out. We are giddy, anticipating how this is going to bless you and Elizabeth. We had this in mind the whole time and thought you'd be delighted by waiting a little longer for a much greater answer than you even asked for. You won the lottery being in the Holy of Holies for this announcement, the ultimate venue. Your response and slowness to get it is underwhelming. For a man in your role, it's stunning you would even suggest God wouldn't or couldn't deliver. We're going to give you some time to think about it in a verbal time-out."

No, Gabriel uses fewer words and is classier in verses 19-20, "I am Gabriel, who stands in the presence of God, and I have been sent to speak to you and to bring you this good news . . . and you shall be silent and unable to speak until the day these things take place, because you did not believe my words, which will be fulfilled in their proper time." So even Zacharias goes agnostic about the voice of God. It's not just us moderns!

THE THREE VOICES

For 13 chapters, we have presented biblical and contemporary stories illustrating God is not silent. He speaks to us in various ways and we've begun to work through our indifference and agnosticism about this. We're observing and practicing 10 characteristics of God's voice to help confirm it is God speaking. How do we discern between God's voice and other voices? Ultimately there are three: God's voice, the voice of the evil one, and our own voices. I wholeheartedly confirm Steve Petermeyer's summary of discerning between God's voice and the evil one's voice. One is loud and accusing; the other is gentle, quieter, and affirming. Our own voices are often easy to identify as they're usually full of doubt or negative thoughts. Jesus, in the midst of saying, "My sheep hear My voice . . ." in John 10, sprinkled in this summation of the battle zone: "The thief comes only to steal, kill and destroy; but I have came that they might have life and have it abundantly." (John 10:10)

THE BATTLE FOR MY DAD

My dad came to faith in Jesus at the age of 51, months before felling a tree that fell on him, breaking his arms and collarbones and crushing his head in. He lived a few days. No one would say my dad was religious, but he was a seeker, mostly paying attention to alternative forms of spirituality. The final months of his life and coming to faith in Jesus are full of wonder. The story is in chapter 11 of our book *Spiritual Seeds*. But it was fraught with spiritual conflict where he was an entrapped POW in the spiritual realm. Several things brought his deliverance to a head, but one incident exposed war-time voices and the tactics of the enemy to keep him captive.

My dad called a psychic hotline. The first call was random. The person he spoke with was random. They knew nothing about him, which made the psychic's comment puzzling, even unnerving. "You've had eight children." Most people thought that he'd had seven children. But the truth was there were eight. Only four people knew about his first child. Freaked out, he immediately called my mom. How could the psychic know something completely buttoned down for over 30 years?

She explained to him that demons have been around a long time and know a lot of stuff. (The movie *Nefarious* brilliantly illustrates this, as does C.S. Lewis's *The Screwtape Letters*.) It would be nothing for the demon information network to share the "Bob" file, seeing the opportunity to put their hooks deeper into his soul as they had him on the ropes. He was desperate. But many were praying for him, and we discovered later that the gentler, affirming voice of Jesus was calling him in many creative ways.

Demon voices use information to accuse and condemn. They offer no hope, redemption, or deliverance. My mom knew those voices too well and lived under their vicious torment until she discovered forgiveness and deliverance in Jesus and the live-in presence of the Holy Spirit. We, her children, saw her pivot. It was her testimony, sharing books, and vigilant prayer that enabled me and others to hear Jesus.

The battle for my dad's life began when he was conceived out of wedlock in the mining and ranching town of Red Lodge, Montana. His birth mother, Mattie, put him up for adoption in the Florence Crittendom Home in Helena, Montana, in 1928. It was what we would call a pregnancy resource center. Unable to have children, Don and Edna Strain were granted the opportunity to adopt Robert Alf and renamed him Robert Donald Strain. They enthusiastically loved him as their own, keeping the adoption a secret from him until he joined the Marines.

If Mattie had been in New York City when Dad's conception occurred in 1928, she may have been guided by another voice to Margaret Sanger's American Birth Control League (founded in 1921), which later became the Planned Parenthood Federation of America. Of course, if that had happened, my dad would not have been around for me to be around, nor my sons and grandsons. Voices and choices have consequences.

LIFE OR DEATH CHOICES

I wondered what my dad would choose if given a death-time option: 1) within the first few months in the womb, or 2) by a falling tree limb at age 51? There is no doubt Don and Edna Strain would choose age 51, as would I and my siblings and most who knew him. Ironically, in later-term abortion procedures, dilation and evacuation procedures are used for 96 percent of abortions performed at 13-plus weeks gestation in the United States. These particularly gruesome surgical techniques involve crushing, dismemberment, and removal of a fetal body from a woman's uterus. Ironically, it includes the crushing of the skull and sucking the brains out for easier removal of the head. Yes, disturbing, but stay focused.

I asked myself, and now imaginatively ask my Dad: "Would you rather have your head crushed by someone who swore the Hippocratic oath while in your mother's womb, or have your head crushed by an oak tree at age 51?" (Believe me, this kind of question would not be out-of-bounds with him.)

The adopted son, Marine, father, cattle rancher, race-horse trainer, and breeder would *no doubt* have chosen age 51. He would choose to live into the danger for a *valuable future*. (It certainly is valuable to his offspring!) His valuable future became more valuable at age 51 when he met Jesus, the eternal King in whose presence he will dwell forever.

His final conversation was to bend his neighbor's ear about how proud he was of his seven children. Then he added, "Now I have one more thing to do—cut down that old oak tree before it falls on my barn." He saved the barn.

VOICES DETERMINE CHOICES

Who are we listening to in the war for true identity and aligning purpose? Our friend, Karen, has been warring for her children, whose identities are being assaulted by every destructive voice imaginable. One day, with praying friends, she asked God, "What do you want me to know about my children?"

She heard in her mind's ear these gentle and affirming words: "They are my children too."

This is the overarching theme of the final chapters.

ASK. THIS. NOW.

PERSONAL REFLECTION AND GROUP DISCUSSION

Was there something in this chapter you were attracted to or challenged by?

With what you've gleaned so far, jot some notes down clarifying the characteristics of the following voices and how you know which is which.

- The evil one's voice: _____
- Your voice: _____
- God's voice: _____

Consider Steve Petermeyer's question, "What if every believer *learned* to hear God?" What if this included children, like Samuel in 1 Sam 3?

Appendix: 10-S Answer Key (page 249)

Chapter 14's 10-S indicators of God's voice will enhance your answers to the Personal Reflection and Group Discussion questions.

GIVE GOD A MINUTE JOURNAL

You Gotta *Ask*	You Gotta Listen & Watch *Answer*
Date:	

15

HEARING HIS VOICE FOR US AND OUR CHILDREN

What if Jesus has been with us our entire lives, even speaking to us in ways we may not have noticed? He was there. Jesus's love for children has major implications for our parenting and helps us to see this God-given privilege in a new light. We predict that when you understand how much the Father loves children, it will bring freedom and light to many parents in a dark night of the soul regarding their children, especially adult children.

ASK AND SEEK

As Pam shares Karen's story, we see many things, especially the 10-S characteristics of hearing God's voice. Watch for these. Also, note that God responds to us in the context of our whole lives in His perfect timing. One thing you'll notice about Karen is she is a seeker in the best sense. "Call to Me and I will answer you, and I will tell you great and mighty things, which you do not know." (Jeremiah 33:3)

"Ask, and it will be given to you; seek and you will find; knock, and it will be opened to you. For everyone who asks receives, and he who seeks finds, and to him who knocks it will be opened . . . If you then, being evil, know how to give good gift to your children, how much more will your Father who is in heaven give what is good to those who ask Him!" (Matthew 7:7-8, 11)

GOD MEETS US WHERE WE ARE

I (Pam) met Karen in May of 2022. Having just moved here, she was looking for connections with other women. When I initially met with Karen, she was *so* open and was looking for meaning and purpose to her life. She knew she wanted to make changes but didn't know how or what. But she did know that somehow it involved spirituality and/or God.

We had multiple conversations and began working through a discussion series I wrote called Investigate. During the course of our discussions, she was very drawn to God's amazing grace and His unconditional love for her. Yet she couldn't fathom that He could accept her and love her in light of all her failures. It sounded amazing, and she was craving it, but just couldn't believe it for herself.

Though Karen had some church background, there was a block. "My head could understand the Bible verses, the cross, etc. It was there, *but I just didn't get it.* But it was Pam's faith and ability to express and live it that enabled me to ask for the same. I began praying and seeking God all the time, reading the Bible and other books."

Fast forward a few months. Karen showed up to my house for a gathering. She told me she had some amazing news to share with me. She was lit up and very animated. "Pam, you will never guess what happened! The answer came in the shower!" She proceeded to tell me as she was getting ready for church that everything suddenly made sense to her while taking a shower!

"All these things began to download into my head: so much love and acceptance, despite all the decisions I had made to live my life in my own strength to this point. I thought it was up to me to figure it all out. But God said, 'I was there for you the whole time and have loved you through all that.'

"Right there in the shower, I fell on my knees bawling. I apologized and asked Him to forgive me. 'I want to be with You,' I said. I saw images of water and of Jesus in a white gown. I was talking back and forth with God in my mind.

"I planned to go to church that morning but hadn't planned on a 40-minute shower, so I was very late. I really wanted to be baptized in front of everyone at church and asked the greeter when I arrived if I could be baptized that morning. They saw how excited I was and asked if I could wait a week." She laughed. "So I got baptized a week later."

HEARING GOD'S VOICE CAN HAPPEN AT ANY TIME

Lately, there has been a lot going on in Karen's family and she has been struggling, feeling like an outsider. I met with her, prayed with her, and connected her to my sister's Boundaries group via Zoom. She felt a huge burden lift.

She offered to volunteer at a LIFT event, so we placed her on the hospitality team. When I first saw her, I could tell by looking at her that she was doing much better. And she took her job seriously in welcoming women.

Karen noticed my neighbor, Debra, walk in alone. She took it upon herself to make sure Debra had someone to sit with and listened to her. Debra's husband had died two years prior, quite suddenly, to cancer, and she was still dealing with profound grief.

Debra and I have different views on some things, but we have had great conversations, and a special bond has formed. I almost didn't ask her to come. Honestly, I was nervous about her coming and not liking what she heard.

I ended up inviting her only three days before the event. I really thought she would say no because it's hard for her to go into public places. She asked me if she would be able to distance herself at the event because the two-year anniversary of her husband's death was coming up. Debra found herself crying a lot. She didn't want to be a bother to anyone and wanted her privacy. I assured her she could do that.

So guess who greeted Debra when she arrived? Karen!

"God guided me over to Debra," Karen explained. "I could tell she was overwhelmed when she shared briefly what she was going through. I don't remember all the words I said, but I just tried loving on her."

Debra later told me she was thinking about leaving, but Karen made the difference and she stayed. "Let's find a place for you to sit where you can grieve if needed, but I'll be sitting right over here if you want company," she told Debra. This was a clear answer to prayer about the event that *every woman would feel loved, seen, and known.*

Karen was loving others as she was being loved by God, my fellow sisters-in-Christ, and me.

GOD'S VOICE IN THE REAL WORLD

As an ultrasound imaging tech, Karen later described to me a mysterious thing happening with her patients. "They start telling me all kinds of things about their lives. I can't believe what they reveal to me. I listen, but often it puts me behind schedule." What was happening? Does seeing inside someone with ultrasound create some kind of trust, making them feel that Karen can see into their soul and spirit too? They feel loved, seen, and known. Perhaps Karen's God-given identity, purpose, and spiritual gift are in operation.

Karen heard God's voice over her family's situation too. After a Boundaries class, my sister, Cindy, prayed with Karen, asking Jesus to speak to the anxiety she was experiencing related to her teenage children.

She heard, "I love you, My daughter. They're My children too. I love them so much."

The Lord your God is with you,
The Mighty Warrior who saves.
He will take great delight in you;
In His love he will no longer rebuke you,
but will rejoice over you with singing.

— Zephaniah 3:17 NIV

ASK. THIS. NOW.

PERSONAL REFLECTION AND GROUP DISCUSSION

Was there something in this chapter you were attracted to or challenged by?

Ask, seek, and *knock* in Matthew 7:7 are present-tense imperative verbs, implying they are commands to be practiced continually. Since parenting is an analogy used in Matthew 7:7-11, we will frame some reflection on having children and being children.

If you have children:

Ask: "Jesus, what do You want me to know about our (Your and my) children? And what do You want me to do? What can I pray for them? How can I love them as You do?"

Seek: "Help me to be watchful for Your answers in my spirit, in Scripture, in counsel from other wise people, and in providential circumstances."

Knock: Write down what He guides you to pray for. Write it someplace you will see it and be prompted to remain watchful. He loves answering your prayers and co-parenting with you. Remember, God's voice is affirming, not condemning. (Matthew 7:9-10; Zephaniah 3:17)

For everyone:

Ask: "Father, am I experiencing You for who You are or am I experiencing You through the filter of deficits in my childhood? What do You want me to know about this?"

Seek: "What do You want me to do about it?"

Knock: *Untying the Knots of the Heart* is a discipleship process presented by Inner Life Ministries. It shows a pathway to work through our dysfunctional or confused childhoods and make a powerful connections with the loving culture in the family of the Trinity: Father, Son, and Holy Spirit. Visit their website: InnerLifeMinistries.org

Appendix: 10-S Answer Key (page 250)

Chapter 15's 10-S indicators of God's voice will enhance your answers to the Personal Reflection and Group Discussion questions.

GIVE GOD A MINUTE JOURNAL

You Gotta *Ask*	You Gotta Listen & Watch *Answer*
Date:	

GOD'S VOICE IS A BLESSING

The voice of God is a blessing. It is not condemnation, accusation, or separation. This doesn't mean that every statement of God is what we want to hear, because to bless another includes instructing, correcting, and reproving. We are often our own worst enemies by ignorance or defiance. It's been this way since Genesis 3 when the original man and woman ignorantly and defiantly side-stepped the command not to eat the fruit of the tree of the knowledge of good and evil. There was a serious consequence, but immediately God put in play a course correction and provision.

God is ever providing and protecting, using all of life to invite us into blessing and abundance, provision, and protection, starting with His presence and guiding voice. But, as satirist Will Rogers said, "There are three kinds of men. The one that learns by reading. The few who learn by observation. The rest of them have to pee on the electric fence for themselves."

LOVING OUR CHILDREN FOR WHO THEY ARE

We just spent four days with our oldest son, Bryant, and his family as they welcomed their third son, Jack, into the world.

Our time was filled with play, work, and food. The overall tone of their family is blessing and affirmation, but childish nonsense needs to be addressed to make this possible. In every activity, the instruction, correction, and reproof were age-appropriate.

Titus, age 6, worked with us, remodeling the family's new home one day. There were things he could do, but there were perils to watch out for: a hole in the floor he about fell through, nails sticking out of old flooring he carried to the debris trailer, and tools he should not touch. But there were ways he could participate, and he was a big help as he listened to the commands of his dad and grandpa. What he learned contributed to his connection with us and the work of restoring the new home to be a place of abundance, security, and livelihood.

Zeke, age 4, was not ready for this activity but received comparable affirmation, instruction, correction, and reproof in his world—mostly playing and picking up toys. Jack, two weeks old, pooped, ate, and slept—all age appropriate. He mesmerized Pop Pop and G-ma. We held him and marveled at the Creation of God with the realization of everything Bryant and Christina went through to bring him into the world.

THE PRIESTLY BLESSING

Bryant and Christina's parenting reminds us to read our Bible in context to see the heart of God in blessing his Creation and children. Do we really believe the priestly blessing of Numbers 6:24-26, or is it wishful sentiment?

> *The Lord bless you and keep you;*
> *The Lord make His face shine on you, and be gracious to you;*

The Lord lift up His countenance on you, and give you peace [shalom: full flourishing].

If He didn't mean it, why would God give the command to Moses for Aaron and his sons to bless the children of Israel, invoking God's name, with the promise of God blessing them? (Num 6:22-23, 27)

ANOTHER AMAZING EXAMPLE

My brother, Kim, recited this priestly blessing before bedtime to each of his 10 birth children and four Liberian adopted children when they were in the home. Few knew this until his funeral. I had no idea and was overwhelmed by the theme of the Father's blessing that ran through his entire service: the songs shared by his children, the messaging through family members who shared, and finally a remarkable poem written by his wife, Heidi. During the reception, the normal slideshow feature was made abnormal by the recurring image of Kim holding each child and grandchild. It was the consistency of his facial expression—satisfaction, contentment, delighting, and being in the moment with each one—that stirred me.

As I mentioned, he had a lot of kids! He and Heidi rivaled Jacob's 12, who I will discuss later in this chapter. One relative who was skeptical of Kim's adoption of Jewish practices and the volume of his family, admitted to me that he misread what was happening. The children embody a relationship with God, community, goodness, hard work, industry, creativity, innovation, and devotion to the family. Kim and Heidi lived together in their royal priesthood identity (1 Peter 2:9), imparting the face of the Father's blessing toward His children.

HIS FACE

Foundational to hearing God's voice is realizing His face is turned toward us, even when we don't deserve it. Like the prodigal father in the Luke 15 parable, Jesus shared, "But while he [the wayward son] was still a long way off, his father saw him and felt compassion for him, and ran and embraced him and kissed him." (Luke 15:20)

Is His face turned toward me? Yes. Longingly. Watchfully. We have to know His face is turned toward us before we can know He is speaking to us. We know we've done wrong, and what we do not need is more accusation, condemnation, separation, and canceling. This is not the Father's posture or voice. This is the enemy's voice. God's voice is invitation, forgiveness, kindness, reconciliation, blessing, liberality, and scandalous grace—all made possible through Jesus and activated daily through the Holy Spirit speaking grace and truth within our hearts.

IN THE ARMS OF MY FATHER

God first came to me in the hug of my own earthly father following a great transgression. With the news of our family selling our ranch and moving to another Montana town, we were upset. The new owners took over putting up the hay since it would be their livelihood in the winter. My older brother and I vandalized their equipment. As a 6-year-old, there was not a lot I could do to heavy metal equipment, but I tried. We did enough to get noticed.

I woke the next morning to find local law enforcement in our kitchen investigating our crime. My brother was doing his best to deflect, deny, and provide decoys to get them off our trail, but facts contradicted his story. Finally, I broke. Saying nothing, I buried my tearful guilty face in my dad's stomach. He simply hugged me. An amazing response from the Marine, Montana cowboy, and disciplinarian who could have turned me away and applied the "board of education" to my "seat of knowledge." Instead, he hugged me, the truly guilty one, his face turned toward me in my shame.

My dad's image is very powerful in my mind's eye, helping me to understand the grace of God. No words were necessary in this case. If my dad could love me like this, how much more could God?

A GIFT AND ITS FRUIT

In a full circle, years later, my upper grade-school son, Jason, and I were sideways about some issue. Neither of us can remember what the issue was. I do recall it was something I was not going to budge on, and he thought I was ridiculously rigid. When I walked out of his bedroom, I felt desperate because I wouldn't budge, and he was not giving me the benefit of the doubt. Worse, he perceived me and my motive in a dark way. I prayed, "Father, what are we going to do with our son, Jason? I don't know what to do with this. How can I let him know I love him in a real way?" Something came into my mind almost immediately—no audible voice, but a tangible thought.

Give him a gift. It's his love language. Buy the gadget he was eyeballing at the discount store. It was a baseball glove gumball machine, a kind of a silly thing, but it seemed like a great idea. It certainly was not expensive. I drove straight over, purchased it, then came home and knocked on his door.

"Jason, I'm sorry we're not seeing eye-to-eye right now. I got you this gift and want you to know I love you, buddy." He received the gift, and I gave him his space. Nothing more was said until several years later, on my 50th birthday. Pam and I were traveling to Rome on a train. She presented me with cards written by many people and a Voice Quilt mp3 file containing voice messages, which I listened to while walking around the Roman Pantheon. Jason was studying abroad in Torino, Italy, but he called in his message before we arrived in Italy. He made some affirming comments, then hung up, only to call again to recount the occasion of our disagreement (whatever it was) and the effect of the gift.

> I remember when I was 9 or 10 years old, and we had a conflict. I was sitting on my bed stewing over it when you returned with the gumballs-in-a-baseball-glove gift and said, "I just want you to know I love you, buddy." I remember that moment so clearly. It was so powerful to me. I have no idea what I was mad at you about but the fact that you took time to go to Kings, buy me the gift (costing only $2-3), knowing it was something I would value—I knew you loved me but *that* really showed it in a way that meant so much to me. I've never said anything about it, but I think about it all the time. It's a cool example of the way you view people, love them, and respect them.

Blown away doesn't capture my reaction. Without question, I was transcended in my desperation. A real dark moment was blown away by the light of God's guiding voice.

In retrospect, it was lit up with the 10-S test:

- ☑ 1. **Scriptural**: Numbers 6:24-26; Luke 15:20, 22; Malachi 4:6
- ☑ 2. **Smarter than you**: I had no idea what to do. I was desperate.
- ☑ 3. **Surprising**: I heard, "Get him a gift," along with exactly what and where to buy.
- ☑ 4. **Specific** (answer to an ask): The answer was almost immediate.
- ☑ 5. **Succinct** (one-liner): "Buy the King's baseball glove gumball machine."
- ☑ 6. **Spot-on** (customized): I knew Jason's love language of gifts.
- ☑ 7. **Spiritually fruitful**: I found out the result years later.
- ☑ 8. **Supported by spiritually gifted people**: It was supported by Pam's Moms in Prayer weekly prayers.
- ☑ 9. **Salvation-minded**: The interaction was foundational to salvation because it broke our separation.
- ☑ 10. **Serving others' best interests**: It served him then and me forever.

GOD USED A DECEIVER AND USURPER

Jacob was willing to deceive his father, Isaac, to receive his blessing. He already manipulated his brother Esau, who was favored by Isaac, out of the birthright at his mother's cunning prompt. From these two instances, we could spend hours unpacking the dysfunction in this family. Jacob felt he was short-changed, being the second-born by minutes, his hand on Esau's heel, as they came out of the birth canal. Jacob means "supplanter," and it became a self-fulfilling prophecy. But it was always the Lord's purpose to bless Abraham's family and through them all the people of the earth. (Genesis 12:1-3, 15, 17, 22, 26; Isaac 28:10-18)

God spoke to Jacob in a dream, confirming His intent to bless him and others through him (Genesis 28:12-14). With his awareness growing of God's presence and intent in his life, Jacob awakened from the dream saying, "Surely the Lord is in this place, and I did not know it." (Genesis 28:16)

But God needed to give him a dose of his own medicine through Laban, his uncle, to burn out the womb-based war in his soul. Years passed in the foreign land while God gave him family and spoke to him in a dream about how to grow his flock and create wealth. He became so prosperous that it made it impossible to live in proximity to his uncle. God spoke again in a dream and directed him to return home to face his brother. (Genesis 31:11-16)

JACOB BECOMES ISRAEL

In the pressure of the situation, Jacob had a showdown wrestling match with God on the journey. He said, "I will not let you go unless you bless me." (Genesis 32:26) He became Israel, the new name God revealed to him, which means "he who wrestles with God." Why? Because he had striven, persevered, and wrestled with God—and prevailed. "And He [God] blessed him there." (Genesis 32:29) Jacob, now Israel, named the place Penial, meaning, "I have seen God face to face yet my life [soul] has been preserved." (Genesis 32:30)

As Will Rogers said, ". . . The rest of them have to pee on the electric fence for themselves." So the Numbers 6:24-26 priestly blessing makes sense to bestow on every child. Really, only God can get to the junk in our souls that keeps us from experiencing His blessing and our true identities and names. But blessing, praying for, and teaching our children to hear God's voice are ways we can partner with God to raise our children—His children. Strangely, He uses our children to strip us of our junk and do through our lives what only God can envision. Jacob had no idea the Messiah would come through the lineage of his son, Judah.

ASK. THIS. NOW.

PERSONAL REFLECTION AND GROUP DISCUSSION

Was there something in this chapter you were attracted to or challenged by?

Like Jacob, are you striving for a father's blessing? What makes you *wrestle* with God about this? Is it time to stop striving and replace it with asking, listening, and receiving? (Psalm 46:10)

Have you started asking, "What is my true name/identity?"

You gotta listen because God speaks to and through all kinds of "Jacobs" on the way to becoming "Israel."

> "But now, thus says the LORD, your Creator, O Jacob, and He who formed you, O Israel, 'Do not fear, for I have redeemed you; I have called you by name; you are Mine!'" (Isaiah 43:1)

> ". . . And you will be called by a new name which the mouth of the LORD will designate." (Isaiah 62:2b)

Appendix: 10-S Answer Key (page 251)

Chapter 16's 10-S indicators of God's voice will enhance answering the Personal Reflection and Group Discussion questions.

GIVE GOD A MINUTE JOURNAL

You Gotta *Ask*	You Gotta Listen & Watch *Answer*
Date:	

NAMES MEAN SOMETHING

When we discovered the ancestry of my dad, who was adopted at birth, we learned the story of how his birth father ended up in Montana. My dad never knew anything about his birth family but discovered that he and his birth father shared a strange commonality.

Alf Miller came west from Minnesota to become a cowboy. During his time in Red Lodge, Montana, he acquired the nickname Buck. When he returned to Hutchinson, Minnesota, he opened a tire store, Buck Miller Tires. The name *Buck* stuck. Likely, he earned it the hard way, taking a tumble or two off the back of bucking horse.

When his son, Robert, was adopted and being raised by my grandparents, Don and Edna, he was put on horseback for the first time. My grandmother told me they were shocked when he took off on the horse like he'd been riding all his life. No fear. He was made for horses; or they were made for each other.

My dad's birth certificate read "Robert Alf" but the Strains renamed him Robert Donald after his new father. He was Don and Edna's only cherished son. His adoption records were sealed and there was no looking back. His identity and belonging were settled. No information was shared with anyone for any reason until my dad enlisted with the Marines. Only then did Edna reveal that he was adopted—but she had no details to share.

"You are our son—chosen, cherished, and loved. Period."

My dad's genetic line (Moller/Miller) goes back to Denmark and the city of Viking kings, Jelling. But we carry the Strain name, in the life-nurturing legacy of Don and Edna.

> **In the Bible, names were given to mark an experience or to emphasize something, such as a transition from an old or false identity to a new one—Abram to Abraham, Jacob to Israel, Simon to Peter, Saul to Paul. The new name broke with the past and ushered in the new, God-given essence.**

NAMES MARK OWNERSHIP OR LEADERSHIP

When one owns or creates something, they gain the authority to name it. When God names or renames something or someone, it signals a new sense of identification and clarified purpose. A name also carries with it a reputation like fame or glory. When God gave Adam dominion over the new Creation, he gave him the privilege of naming the living creatures. (Gen 2:19-20) And he named his wife, Eve, signaling leadership. (Gen 3:20)

NAMES HAVE EVERYTHING TO DO WITH IDENTITY AND RELATIONSHIP

Of a restored Israel, God said, "The nations will see your righteousness, and all kings your glory; and you will be called by a new name which the mouth of the Lord will designate." (Isaiah 62:2)

When God spoke to the descendants of Israel, He reminded them of their identity and who owns and calls them into being. Jacob, meaning "heel-holder" or "supplanter," was renamed Israel, "one who prevails with God," by God. Isaiah writes, "But now, thus says the LORD, your Creator, O Jacob, and He who formed you, O Israel, 'Do not fear, for I have redeemed you; I have called you by name; you are Mine!'" (Isaiah 43:1)

God satisfied Jacob's lifelong pursuit of a father's blessing and gave him a memorial name that his descendants would ponder and use to calibrate their own lives. Their struggle for significance and blessing would likewise be found in their Creator and Redeemer God. When they passed through the flood waters and fires of tribulation, they too found their lives in the identity and presence of God (Isaiah 43:2-7) and became His witnesses (Isaiah 43:10-13).

WILL GOD SPEAK TO YOU ABOUT YOUR ESSENCE BY GIVING YOU A NEW NAME?

You gotta ask, "Father, what do You call me?" Then, you gotta give Him a minute and listen.

And we shouldn't stop there. Isaiah says we are to bear witness, starting with the next generation, inviting others to hear His voice as well. Consider the beautiful story of our friends Drayth and DeAnne Sielaff.

Drayth read through Jamie Winship's book *Fearless Living*. He felt called to read through the book with his wife and youngest daughter to recreate the same opportunity for his family to hear God, similar to the opportunity Jamie provided 300 men in Salt Lake City. Jamie used the book as a template to guide the men to discover their names. Drayth and DeAnne devoted 9 to 10 hours over a couple days to accomplish this with their daughter, Ashlyn. Ashlyn had just graduated from high school and was timidly pondering the vast terrain of her whole life going forward. They knew how overwhelmed she was and sensed her paralysis about moving out because she didn't have a purpose or idea of what God wanted her to be. Their format for these few hours was to read and/or listen to the audiobook, discuss it, eat, and take a break—then repeat as needed.

On Friday, during the prayers recorded in the book, DeAnne heard God whisper to her, "Homemaker." Those who know DeAnne best would think, "Of course!"

Drayth heard, "Compassionate Servant Leader; Anointed Musician." I've known the details of Drayth's adult life, ministry, and effect well over 20 years. I thought, "Yes! Right on!" when I heard this. It resonated with Drayth, but now he is seeking God about how it will play out.

Ashlyn heard nothing on Friday, but they encouraged her to keep listening for there was no hurry. Ashlyn honestly confessed, "God, I don't think I'll hear from you." But she stayed the course. Ashlyn is not a breakfast person, but they went to a small breakfast joint to start Saturday's reading experience. While eating, she started smiling and said to her parents,

"I think I just heard from God." Ashlyn heard, "Fashion and Modeling for Jesus."

Recounting this, Drayth told me, "That makes so much sense. Years prior, when we were attempting to purchase basketball shorts for her, it took forever to choose. She was so picky. They had to be just right. 'But Ashlyn, they're just basketball shorts! It doesn't matter,' I would plead. Thankfully, after looking at multiple stores, we finally found something that would work."

Ashlyn has always been drawn to making and designing clothing, especially jeans. After she learned how to sew, she inherited her grandmother's sewing machine. With her God-given name in mind, she found a mentor, Cathy. Cathy's daughter was a designer of clothing who sold her designs on Instagram. Ashlyn is beginning to live out her essence and her name with big energy. She is transformed. Drayth and DeAnne had been full of awe, wonder, and concern for her future, but that has turned into eager anticipation of what God has in store for Ashlyn.

Drayth and DeAnne's other daughter, Prestyn, and their son-in-law, Chris, are educators at a Christian school in the Portland region. Chris instructs students in science and leads a Bible study class for senior boys, while Prestyn teaches music and art and oversees a Bible study class for senior girls. They found Winship's messages about identity, purpose, and the future particularly relevant for their senior students contemplating life after high school. Pam and I had the opportunity to hear about their experiences firsthand. The teachings resonated with nearly all the students; they felt that God communicated with them personally, revealing their divine names. There were two students who did not have this experience, but they were encouraged to remain open to hearing from God, trusting His timing. Chris has been so inspired by these events that he is in the process of writing a book about the experience.

BEING AN ADVOCATE FOR OTHERS

God speaks to and through all kinds of people. As God told our friend, Karen, "They're My kids too." The good news is that He has been speaking to us all our lives. But like many, we simply don't know to listen to Him, or how to listen at all. So many of us had no one instructing us how to respond to God, like Eli to young Samuel: "Speak Lord, your servant is listening." Like Eli in 1 Samuel 3, Drayth, DeAnne, Prestyn, and Chris stepped into their royal priesthood identities as the King's advocates, teaching others how to respond and listen to what God is saying.

Can you think of anything our children and our entire culture need more than to hear their names and identities from God Himself? But who is there to prompt the idea and guide them in the process? God is there and He is not silent. He invites each of us to come to him in truth and trust, realness and faith. When someone's God-given identity is named, they gain the ability to grow and expand into their identity, purpose, and mission.

The only other option is to live as a victim in a false or pseudo-identity with shame, guilt, anger, and fear. We can never get from other humans what only God can give. Identity is not circumstantial; it's God-breathed. The lie is that we are stuck in victimhood. But the truth that God is speaking is we can choose a different response to the life events that have chipped away and pulverized our essential God-given identities and worth. If we can hear His names for us, everything will change.

So, what do you want for yourself and those you care about?

Option 1: The road most traveled leaves you blaming others for your woes and thus, makes you isolate yourself more and more. On this path, one day you find yourself alone, still lost, still angry, and trapped in fear.

Option 2: The road less traveled find you taking God's hand as He speaks truth and life to you in the present and answers the lies from the past that have cut deep wounds in your soul.

Option two may require going back in your mental history to speak to yourself as a child at points of deep hurt. Why? Because Jesus, the sovereign one and healer, was there—not bound by time. Wherever you are on your timeline, He is there.

JESUS AS THE GREATEST COUNSELOR

Consider my historical event described below and the quirky but deeply healing encounter I had with God recently. One might do this with a therapist, but in my case, the Spirit of Jesus was my real-time counselor.

Aged 9, I was seated in the middle of my dad's truck, on the front bench seat, Dad behind the wheel, my brother on the right. We had finished the daily tasks of exercising the racehorses, cleaning stalls, etc. and were eating lunch. Stick-shift between my legs, I held a bologna and cheese sandwich in my right hand and Styrofoam cup of Tang, official drink of the astronauts, in my left. Contentedly eating, my dad dropped a bomb seemingly out of nowhere. It would change the lives of the seven Strain children for a lifetime.

"Should I tell him now?" my dad asked my brother. My brother shrugged his shoulders and looked out the window. With a knot in the pit of my stomach, I thought, *Uh-oh! What's going on here?*

"Your mother and I are not going to be married anymore."

I said nothing because I couldn't absorb it. The question in my mind was "How is it even possible that you cannot be married anymore?" Wordless, I began to sob. My little 9-year-old body shook as I tried not to spill the official drink of the astronauts. It's still a vivid memory.

A book could be written about the consequences, but I'll summarize it in a paragraph or two. Starting that day, I believed a lie that would unconsciously guide me for many years. "You can only count on you. Everyone and everything you care about will go away, be taken away, or die. You can only count on you." I've had to stare this lie in the face my entire life. Self-reliance became an unseen but growing force in my identity. With self-reliance comes a complementary message, "You gotta get out of here." It explained my acting out, getting into a bit of trouble on various fronts. It explained how I felt emasculated when not with my dad.

My only solution was self-reliance. I wanted to be in my dad's exciting world of work, horse racing, competition, earning our livelihoods, and becoming a man. Instead, I was "stuck" in my mom's world of church—children, moms, old people, and a few boring men—and without adventure. "I gotta get out of here." Because of this feeling, summers during grade school were largely spent with my dad. In high school, I always found summer jobs somewhere away from home in Montana, working with my brother, Kim. I went reptilian-minded, trying to survive the bomb of my parents' divorce through sports and work, which became my lonely pseudo-identity. Then, thankfully, a miracle reset my life when I met Jesus at age 18. With Him came boundless resources. He was the loving Father, leader, and companion who would be with me forever.

WHERE WAS JESUS WHEN THE BOMB EXPLODED?

At age 63, a new thought occurred to me. Where was Jesus that day in the truck when the bomb went off? It had never occurred to me before that I could ask Him. So I did. I decided to wait quietly for Him to respond.

Sitting at a table in my home, I recalled the day of the bomb and without warning began sobbing just like the day I heard my dad's words. In a holy and raw place, I opted for the privacy of our back yard so I wouldn't have to explain the sobbing to Pam if she overheard me. Still feeling the grief from that day, I began pulling weeds, cleaning the yard, and picking up golf balls while waiting for the voice of Jesus. I don't know what I expected to hear—"I was sitting on the stick shift," or "I was hanging from the mirror"—but I asked and waited.

As I was kneeling down over the garden box, something prompted me to look behind me. Startled, I wondered why the neighbor's cat was sitting on the irrigation box five yards away. It surprised me because he doesn't usually come close to me. I'm always running him out of our garage or off our deck where he once puked in front of our sliding door. "Get out of here, ya dumb cat!"

Almost simultaneously, in my inner ear, I heard, "I was with you in the animals."

With the statement came mental film footage from the life of young Jon and his immersion in animals during what I think of as the dark season. The film included two cats who had litters of kitties we played with—I actually liked cats once. It included our cattle dog, Cindy, whose employment was reduced to home protector, car chaser, and Jon's buddy. She was largely out of a job working cattle with my dad. Both of us were disenfranchised—her presence provided a form of empathy and continuity of good things past. Together, we absorbed the losses.

Then there were the horses. My dad had a bunch in training during any given summer, up to 24 one summer, and after cleaning stalls while they exercised, I would visit every one of them every day. You could say I had a personal relationship with each horse in Dad's stable. I messed around with them, petting and carrying on until they tired of me. Then I'd move on to the next. My favorite was a filly we called Ida, registered name Ida Winall. And "win all" she did, complemented by her beautiful temperament. She was hands-down my favorite among my dad's stable.

Eventually, injuries ended her racing days, and my dad sent her home to breed to our stud. Her first foal was named Ike. Colts are usually skittish and hard to pet. Not Ike. He was like a dog, completely unafraid of human contact and affectionate. I've never met a colt like him. I think his disposition was a gift from God to me during this time. It was no surprise that, registered under the name Freedom Cup, Ike won a lot of races and was a bread-and-butter runner for my dad.

"I was with you in the animals." This idea introduces the next chapter about how God speaks to us through Creation, including animals. We must realize God speaks to us through all of Creation and has throughout our lives.

ASK. THIS. NOW.

PERSONAL REFLECTION AND GROUP DISCUSSION

Was there something in this chapter you were attracted to or challenged by?

What are you hearing from God about your name?

If you've heard, how do you think it will affect your purpose?

False identities and false narratives come out of trauma. Have you ever invited Jesus to visit a memory that blew you up and you chose to listen to a lie that separated you from Him? "Jesus, where were you when _____?"

Appendix: 10-S Answer Key (page 252)

Chapter 17's 10-S indicators of God's voice will enhance your answers to the Personal Reflection and Group Discussion questions.

GIVE GOD A MINUTE JOURNAL

You Gotta *Ask*	You Gotta Listen & Watch *Answer*
Date:	

18

PLAN TOGETHER

"We plan, God laughs," says the old Yiddish proverb. Building on this, filmmaker and satirist Woody Allen said, "If you want to make God laugh, tell him about your plans." God speaks to and through all kinds of people about our plans when we call on Him. Yet, there are things more important we should be aware of. It's unnerving when we hear only crickets, static, or noise.

We said it already, but just to be clear, God speaks to us about our identities and then our purposes. When our purposes are clarified, we can make plans. But remember that in the midst of *our* plans, God has plans for us (Jeremiah 29:11) and good works in mind that spring forth from the workmanship He creatively performs in us. (Ephesians 2:10) The main idea here is that He is with us in the midst of all of it. Amazingly, He allows us space to be co-creators with Him. Given His powerful and loving position, it's a solid idea to include Him in all of our thoughts, deliberations, and actions, starting with identity. He doesn't speak to false self or false identity—He knows our true identities because He created us.

SHOULD WE EVEN PLAN?

Every year I write a strategic plan and very much understand what Woody Allen's God-laughing-at-our-plans humor is about. We have no idea what the best things will be in the coming year. When I reflect back on a given year, I realize the best things that happened were nowhere on my radar. Plus, the plans we have rarely come to pass because they are surpassed by God's creativity and timely intervention.

The real question is should we take the time to plan at all? Why not just walk with God moment by moment and let it come? The answer is yes, we should plan but also be open for God's timely change of plans. Part of the answer has to do with the fact that we collaborate with others, organizing and using resources. It's a dynamic tension.

Recently, the You Gotta Ask Board engaged in the process of identifying strategic initiatives with a very gifted man named David Alexander. We identified six initiatives for the next few years of our organization. My left brain (logical, rational, factual) understood the process and the good sense these made. My right brain (intuitive, imaginative) was stressing out. I felt trapped, like I was suffocating with obligation to do something I wasn't enthused about and that God might not be in. We had been praying about our process and taking time to arrive at these plans together. Certainly, this honored God. So I asked, "Why, Father, is this stressing me out? Something is incongruent and producing dread in me. This is not what I feel called to, but it makes good sense. What do I need to know? What do I do about this?"

THE ANSWER

God speaks to some of us in dreams. He did this with busy young Solomon (1 Kings 3) who was under a lot of pressure to fill the big shoes of King David, his father. I suspect sleep is a time God can get the attention of many of us through gentle whispers, when some of us are in a restful receiving state.

In my sleep one night, the distinctive name of James O. Fraser was deposited in my mind in a succinct and sticky way. Normal dreams are slippery to hang on to, but this one came out of nowhere and I remembered the name when I woke up. I was impressed to chase it the next morning. It had been a few years since I'd even thought about James O. Fraser. Google the name and you will find Fraser highly quotable on the topic of prayer. But there was one story the Holy Spirit wanted to bring afresh to my attention in answer to my prayer. Working on my master of divinity at Western Seminary, I learned about Fraser during a course on the history of Christian missions. He was a contemporary with Hudson Taylor in China.

As I recall the story, a fellow missionary came to his residence discouraged and defeated. All evening he poured out his burden on a listening Fraser. Finally, he wore himself out and went to bed. He awoke the next morning to find Fraser up.

In paraphrase, Fraser said, "What you shared with me last evening was such a heavy burden that I stayed up all night praying for you. Here is what God impressed on me to say to you this morning. If this is your ministry, the sooner it dies the better. If it's God's ministry, realize He can do more in the snap of a finger than a missionary can in a lifetime of service."

"Many plans are in a man's heart, but the counsel of the Lord will stand." (Proverbs 19:21)

"The mind of man plans his way, but the LORD directs His steps." (Proverbs 16:9)

If God can communicate with me by mixing or combining spiritual thoughts with spiritual words (1 Corinthians 2:13b), why can't He work through us to plan our way by directing our steps organizationally? Paul goes on to say, "But we have the mind of Christ." (1 Corinthians 2:16b)

God revealed to me that He can still direct and change the course of our ministry, even when we have made plans. He reminded me that together is better. It takes intentionality to ask God questions together, watching for his guidance and answers.

CALL UPON ME AND I WILL BE FOUND BY YOU

To the collective exiles in Babylon, God said, "'For I know the plans that I have for you,' declares the LORD, 'plans for welfare and not for calamity to give you a future and a hope. Then you will call upon Me and come and pray to Me, and I will listen to you. You will seek Me and find Me when you search for Me with all your heart. I will be found by you . . .' declares the LORD . . ." (Jeremiah 29:11-14a) Realize that God made this promise to His people while disciplining them for their sustained disobedience.

SOLOMON'S BIG MISTAKE

It was Solomon's inattentiveness to listening in the long run that led to a divided heart and eventually a divided nation. It resulted in Babylonian exile. Solomon's rule started well when God asked Solomon in a dream what he needed to rule well. Solomon's answer was "a hearing heart." God was delighted to deliver the wisdom Solomon would need to shepherd Israel, plus unsurpassed influence. Yet, in the 40 years of his reign we see all kinds of compromise in the face of the Deuteronomy warning Him against foreign wives with false gods; wealth; and weapons of military might, symbolized by horses.

Proactively, Moses gave instructions for the kings of Israel to safeguard their hearts by writing "a copy of the law on a scroll in the presence of the Levitical priests. [19] It shall be with him and he shall read it all the days of his life, that he may learn to fear the Lord his God, by carefully observing all the words of this law [of God] and these statutes, [20] that his heart may not be lifted up above his countrymen and he may not turn aside from the commandment, to the right or the left, so that he and his sons may continue long in his kingdom in the midst of Israel." (Deuteronomy 17:18-20)

You gotta keep asking *and* you gotta keep listening to the written and living Word, together with the community God provides. Where were the Levitical priests during Solomon's reign to safeguard the king's choices and actions with respect to the law of God?

Today, kings and priests are brought together in Christ. Peter says we are a "Kingdom of priests" in community, called the body of Christ. (1 Peter 2:5-9) Together is better because we have the mind of Christ, dwelt in each of us by the Holy Spirit, to move into our true identities, heaven-given purposes, and God-ordained works and plans.

ASK. THIS. NOW.

PERSONAL REFLECTION AND GROUP DISCUSSION

Was there something in this chapter you were attracted to or challenged by?

Inventory:

Who is your current "Kingdom of priests" Christ-community? (Perhaps your struggle with identity and your purpose is not identifying with these people.) Ask, seek, and knock.

Are you hearing God about your true identity first, then discussing His purpose for you that comes out of this identity?

Are your plans built more around the true you co-laboring with God and others, or more a pseudo-you, where you are always self-promoting and self-protecting?

Appendix: 10-S Answer Key (page 253)

Chapter 18's 10-S indicators of God's voice will enhance your answers to the Personal Reflection and Group Discussion questions.

GIVE GOD A MINUTE JOURNAL

You Gotta *Ask*	You Gotta Listen & Watch *Answer*
Date:	

HOW GOD SPEAKS

John Jensen, who had exclusive homeowner access to a stretch of the Big Wood River in Ketchum, Idaho, invited me to fly-fish. He had access to a special spot with a nice deep channel. Add to this his lifetime of fly-fishing practice and an invitation to fish under his watchful eye and instruction, well, how could I say no? This was my first experience using a hopper dropper—a two-fly setup for fly-fishing. John Jensen told me, "When you see the indicator fly bob below, it means there's a fish on the line. So you have to watch and tug the line when you see it drop."

After more instruction about where to cast and how to systematically work the channel by moving my casts around, I began. Twenty minutes later, out of the blue, John said, "Fish on. Pull your line tight."

I looked at him skeptically and said, "I don't feel anything." In my life experience with fishing, I knew I needed to feel the tug of a fish on the line. This time, I didn't feel anything.

John insisted, "No, really. You have a fish on."

I kept casting and missing the prompts. "Isn't that just the bobbing of the waves making the surface fly go out of sight?" I asked.

"It's a fish," he responded, starting to sound a little exasperated. Why wouldn't I simply believe him? My lifelong fishing experience said to cast, mend the line, and leave the fly in the water as long as possible, waiting for the tug. If there was no tug, then I'd re-cast. John was telling me to watch the indicator fly bob, then tug.

Finally, I awkwardly took him at his word and lifted the line when I saw the indicator bob. It was counter-intuitive. *Oh my gosh, I got a fish! He's telling me the truth!* Partially bought-in, I continued trying for consistency with this new method, but being a creature of habit, I had to be re-convinced. At the end of the experience, I was amazed at how many fish I caught standing in one spot casting into one channel. I was equally amazed at how difficult it was to remember to keep doing what master fisherman John Jenson told me to do.

TRUSTING THE EXPERT

All I had to do was listen and respond to the instruction of the expert, who knew there was a channel full of hungry fish and when they were biting on a fly. This story has many parallels with fishing for men, but there is only one I want to make in this chapter. We need to listen to the Master and do what He says with every setup of what to cast, where to cast, and how to watch for indicators. Here are the Biblical assumptions:

1. God is speaking to people about Jesus.
2. God is speaking to us to get our lines in the water with setup and casting instructions for each situation.

3. God gives us the indicators and counsel we need to know about the activity of the fish.
4. We simply need to show up, listen, and respond to what He says. As another friend says, "Quit whining and keep your fly in the water."

Beyond the rich evangelism metaphor, this was a rich spiritual experience in Creation. In fishing and a multitude of other outdoor activities, God speaks through every part of Creation. It's not as specific as words, but people are made to experience God and the proclamation of who God is in Creation. It's not uncommon to hear anyone say things like these:

"God speaks to me in Creation."

"My church is being out in Creation."

These are things I've heard most of my life living in Montana, Utah, and Idaho.

CREATION'S SILENT VOICE

And God is silently vocal through what He has made. Psalm 19:1-6 testifies to it: the heavens are "declaring," "proclaiming," and "pouring forth speech," (19:1-2) but they use "no speech," "[no] words," and "[no] voice." (19:3) Paraphrasing, he says their [noiseless] voice goes out into all the earth and their words to the ends of the world. (19:4)

Creation, from glorious sunrise to glorious sunset, is silent but powerfully proclaims God's glory. Psalm 19:7-13 testifies that natural revelation is complemented with special revelation, namely God speaking through specific words, including the words of His law given through Moses, the Psalms and prophets, Jesus, His apostles, and His understudies.

In You Gotta Ask, we invite people to answer this compelling question: "Assuming there's a God and you can ask God any question, or take God to task on an issue, what would your question or topic be?"

This was mine for a few years: "God, why are you so obscure? Why not be more obvious?" C.S. Lewis helped me the most with answering this question in *The Screwtape Letters*. A mentor demon, Screwtape, explains to his demon-disciple, Wormwood, that there are two tools God cannot use:

1. *God cannot be irresistible.* (He could overwhelm us with beauty itself, but this wouldn't bring us into His love or the reality of our fallenness.)
2. *God cannot be irrefutable.* (He could debate us into submission.)

So God leaves breadcrumbs to invite us to seek, but doesn't overwhelm us. He allows us to get a wafting sniff of His bakery to increase curiosity and watchfulness. Creation is the smell of the bakery. Mmmm, I want more of that. The breadcrumbs are the Gospel of grace packaged in human lives. Smell is a bit ambiguous, but powerful. Snack samples on the trail bring us to the real bakery to meet the baker himself.

HOW GOD HAS BEEN SPEAKING TO US ALL OUR LIVES: PSALM 19 AND ROMANS 1

My hermeneutics professor in graduate school, Dr. Earl Radmacher, assigned the class to memorize Psalm 19. He wanted us to understand the three ways God speaks: 1) Creation (Psalm 19:1-6), 2) His Word, the Torah (Psalm 19:7-10), and 3) our moral consciences. (Psalm 19:11-14)

The first is referred to as general revelation and the second as special revelation. General revelation is constant for the person who connects in any way with created things, starting with the sunrise and sunset. Special revelation uses words, and we must open a book, tool, or device that contains specific words. Finally, moral order is built into all of us. We understand that there is right and wrong.

Note how the descriptive words and images are highlighted in the three ways God speaks in Psalm 19.

General Revelation in Creation:

The heavens are telling of the glory of God;
And their expanse is declaring the work of His hands.
Day to day pours forth speech,
And night to night reveals knowledge.
There is no speech, nor are there words;
Their voice is not heard.
Their line has gone out through all the earth,
And their utterances to the end of the world.
In them He has placed a tent for the sun,
Which is as a bridegroom coming out of his chamber;
It rejoices as a strong man to run his course.
Its rising is from one end of the heavens,
And its circuit to the other end of them;
And there is nothing hidden from its heat.

What do you make of the "telling," "declaring," and "speech," even though there is no speech, words, or voice heard?

How expansive is the wordless proclamation?

What do a bridegroom coming out of his chamber and a strong man running his course say about the vitality of God's communication?

Is there anything untouched by God's communication in Creation?

Can we summarize how God has been speaking to all of us, and all of Creation, throughout our lives?

Special Revelation in Scripture

The law of the Lord is perfect, restoring the soul;
The testimony of the Lord is sure, making wise the simple.
The precepts of the Lord are right, rejoicing the heart;
The fear of the Lord is clean, enduring forever;
The judgments of the Lord are true; they are righteous altogether.
They are more desirable than gold, yes,
than much fine gold;
Sweeter also than honey and the drippings of the honeycomb.

The Torah/law carries the image that points the clear way to the path of life. What are the various words used to describe it and their corresponding effects?

Moral Revelation in Our Consciences

Moreover, by them Your servant is warned;
In keeping them there is great reward.
Who can discern his errors? Acquit me of hidden faults.
Also keep back Your servant from presumptuous sins;

Let them not rule over me;
Then I will be blameless,
And I shall be acquitted of great transgression.
Let the words of my mouth and the meditation of my heart
Be acceptable in Your sight,
O Lord, my rock and my Redeemer.

What are some of the words the Psalmist uses to testify of our moral conscience and that they are either missing or hitting the mark?

THE REPEATED TRI-FOLD PATTERN OF GOD'S COMMUNICATION IN ROMANS 1

Special Revelation in Scripture from Romans 1:

Like Psalm 19:7-10, Romans 1:14-18 is about the Gospel of life, words coming from the righteous nature of God characterized by love, grace, holiness, truth, and justice.

> *I am under obligation both to Greeks and to barbarians, both to the wise and to the foolish. So, for my part, I am eager to preach the gospel to you also who are in Rome.*

> *For I am not ashamed of the gospel, for it is the power of God for salvation to everyone who believes, to the Jew first and also to the Greek.*

> *For in it the righteousness of God is revealed from faith to faith; as it is written, "But the righteous man shall live by faith."*

For the wrath of God is revealed [present tense verb] from heaven against all ungodliness and unrighteousness of men who suppress the truth in unrighteousness.

Moral Revelation in Our Consciences

Like Psalm 19:11-14, Romans 1:19 (elaborated in 1:21-2:16; 3:9-19) speaks of and to our moral consciences.

Because that which is known about God is evident within them; for God make it evident to them.

General Revelation in Creation

Like Psalm 19:1-6, Romans 1:20 speaks of God's communication through Creation. He is constantly testifying and revealing Himself in very subtle, but powerful ways—if we will notice.

For since the creation of the world His invisible attributes, His eternal power and divine, have been clearly seen, being understood through what has been made, so that they are without excuse.

ANOTHER JOHN WHO LOVES CREATION

Let me introduce you to a second fly-fishing mentor and good friend, John Meyer, who lives in Eagle, Idaho.

No one is more aware of this three-fold communication of God than John. He told me, "God has been speaking to me all my life, but I didn't know it for many years because I was running at the speed of light trying to survive my life in business, church, and then raising a family." He can regale a group of men with high school stories of fast cars, hard drinking, and jail. In this he tested the perimeter of his moral conscience, but all the while loving Creation and was exposed to hearing the Scripture.

John Meyer has been hearing God's voice all his life, but has come to realize this most vividly in his 60s. "I grew up in Bakersfield, California, and gained a love of the outdoors hunting and fishing with my dad. My dad made me feel safe. I used to cut pictures out of *Field and Stream* magazine and put them up on my wall. I had a dream as a kid that I'd move to Idaho, and I didn't know what it was, let alone where it was." In these things, God was speaking to John Meyer at a young age.

As an adult, John talked his brother into expanding the business by John moving his family to Idaho. Equally motivating was to get outdoors more with his family and Idaho offered ample immediate access. As a side business, John started a hobby company, putting together wildlife calendars that boomed into something that would employ both his sons. "I started with the first-ever mule deer calendar, then expanded everything else including my main passion, fresh and saltwater fly-fishing. I merged the outdoor calendar business with our pump parts business, handing out outdoor calendars to clients, mostly tough guys who loved the outdoors."

John did much of his own photography, especially fish, which served as a business write-off for his hobby. John invited me (Jon) to float the Grand Ronde River with him and his fly-fishing mentor, Kent Goodman, in a drift boat that a company *gave him* to feature in his calendars. Isn't God good to John? And to me through John?

John Meyer lives for things like fishing "the hatch" at Silver Creek in Sun Valley or the South Fork of the Boise River. He fills in as a guide at a week-long men's camp in Montana and is always mentioned as the highlight of the week. He's a good teacher in the morning, but he loves getting out alone in the afternoon to enjoy the quiet voice of God in Creation. "I marvel at the beautiful paint job God did on every fish— the colors and arrangement, each unique. I never tire of holding these masterpieces. As our friend Ben Bost says, "We are chasing a masterpiece in a masterpiece."

Whether fishing trout in Idaho freshwater or saltwater-fishing in Mexico, John is a curious student of ecosystems, fish, and matching flies to the situation. Anytime he comes upon a body of water, he asks himself, "I wonder where the fish would be in this pool?" The answer is where there are food and high oxygen, there are fish.

BECOMING A FISHER OF MEN

During a trip to Israel, John Meyer was in the wilderness by a pool fed by two streams. "Where would the fish be?" he wondered. He heard a voice in his mind's ear, "That's where you need to be, where there's food and oxygen in your fishing for men."

John pondered this message from God and reflected, "Things go better with Jesus and those who live in His word. Stay with the wife of your youth and honoring her, and things will go better. Make money but give a lot away, and things will go better. Hold positions of power in business and on church and nonprofit boards [Send Hope in India and You Gotta Ask], but be humble, surrender, serve, trust, and let Jesus guide, and things will go better. Jesus is the feeder stream. You don't need to chase your tail around the pond.

Cast your line where the feeder stream creates immediate food and oxygen."

A few days later, John combined a fly-fishing trip in Cuba with an outreach effort serving a local church in Cuba, going home to home to share the Gospel of Jesus. Each day, with a local host, the team of 12 divided up for pre-arranged meetings. Cubans love meeting Americans and want to hear their stories and the Gospel. For a week, John cast his line, home to home, sharing a two- to three-minute version of his testimony imbedded with four verses summarizing the Gospel: God's love; how we fall short; the forgiveness available in Christ; and the chance to receive Jesus. In his story, John Meyer shared that he tried life without Jesus as a young man and it landed him in jail a couple of times. He shared how he lacked purpose but he eventually heard God ask, "Do you want to exchange this for a life with Me?"

As John was sharing with me about how his trip went, he admitted, "Each day, 9 to 11 a.m. and 1 to 4 p.m., I learned to get better at my Gospel cast. Day one, I was too heavy on story. Day two, I was too heavy on Gospel. Day three was finally a good balance."

At the end of the week, 200 households heard about Jesus with 150 people receiving Christ.

John was so encouraged by his trip to Cuba that he asked, "Lord, make me bold in Idaho. Why am I not doing it in Idaho more? What do You want me to do at home?"

He heard, "Start with your grandkids." John Meyer has a lot of grandkids and takes them hunting and fishing. He shares with them about the gift that God has given him. And the gift goes on.

ASK. THIS. NOW.

PERSONAL REFLECTION AND GROUP DISCUSSION

Was there something in this chapter you were attracted to or challenged by?

Psalm 19 and Romans 1 are passages highlighting God's lifetime proclamation to everyone through Creation, our moral consciences, and the Gospel message. John Meyer engages in and embodies all three. Checkmark each of his statements you resonate with:

- ☐ "If it's real, we better be sharing it with others."

- ☐ "Things go better with Jesus and those who live in His word."

- ☐ "I have an ordinary, average, and blessed life. God wants to develop a deeper relationship with me through what I love [outdoors, fly-fishing, and hunting] and more fishing for men."

- ☐ "[Lord] Why am I not doing it [sharing Jesus] at home in Idaho more?" He heard, "Start with your grandkids."

- ☐ "Where would the fish be?" John wondered. He heard a voice in his mind's ear, "That's where you need to be, where there's food and oxygen in your fishing for men."

☐ He heard from God, "Jesus is the feeder stream. You don't need to chase your tail around the pond. Cast your line where the feeder stream creates immediate food and oxygen."

What do you learn from the two fly-fishing Johns (Jenson and Meyer) about seeing the stream of life differently? Are you, like Jon Strain, slow to learn there are hungry fish and there would be "fish on" if you would cast and tug the line?

Appendix: 10-S Answer Key (page 254)

Chapter 19's 10-S indicators of God's voice will enhance your answers to the Personal Reflection and Group Discussion questions.

GIVE GOD A MINUTE JOURNAL

You Gotta *Ask*	You Gotta Listen & Watch *Answer*
Date:	

IT'S YOUR TURN

After reading the Introduction of *You Gotta Listen*, my longtime friend and board member John Meyer said, "You should have written this book before writing *You Gotta Ask*."

"I get what you're saying, John. In fact, two chapters in *You Gotta Ask* are the seedbed for *You Gotta Listen*. While writing them, I questioned myself on this because hearing God is foundational. But I simply wasn't ready. God had much more to say to me. Now I better understand that asking and listening are a beautiful complement, one energizing the other in a cyclical way."

Asking and listening to God's answers should stimulate more and better asking. I've committed to the practice of this and consequently enjoy many fascinating encounters with other people's asking-and-hearing-God stories.

While writing this chapter, Pam had another meeting with her Women of Valor group, who are committed to this very posture. When I asked her how her group went that evening, she lit up, reporting the various encounters her groupies shared just in the past few days. I thought I was listening to the book of Acts.

One of the women audaciously prayed the following on the way to work: "Lord, I haven't shared the Gospel lately. Would you bring someone into my path today to share the Gospel with?"

Seriously? Who prays that? Should we be surprised one of the women on her team approached her that day and asked, "Are you a Christian?" As they explored why she asked the question, she expressed desire to move toward reading the Bible and other ways to move toward God.

Then our friend asked her co-worker, "Where do you think this is coming from?"

She said, "I don't know, I'm just feeling a tug." She is now experiencing resources and guidance in her search for God.

We call this Acts 29. You may know the fifth book of the New Testament, titled "The Acts of the Apostles," has 28 chapters. Acts 29 refers to the rest of God's acts through people in church history to the current day. Likewise, this final chapter of this book is intended to spur us on within the larger context of Acts 29. You are equipped and sent to live, record, and share your stories. With heightened watchfulness and curiosity, you will ask others if they have stories of hearing God. If they claim they haven't, your simple curiosity will heighten their wonder and openness to the possibility God has been speaking to them all their lives. Better, He still is.

The following text from my new friend Aaron arrived as I was writing this chapter:

"It's been on my heart for a while to invite unbelievers and those who are seeking truth into a safe environment where the deep questions of life and of God can be discussed. It could be at a coffee shop, a park, or wherever. Is that something that you would be interested in doing together?

"My idea is to have a setting where strangers could come to question and to seek. Then those people who are interested in taking the next step could be invited into men's and women's groups. Do you think that's feasible, and if so, do you have any ideas on how to get something like at started?"

I said, "Father, would You keep sending people like Aaron my way? Let's multiply the Aarons among Your people!" I cannot wait to prayerfully figure this out with him. I have some ideas and they are based in *You Gotta Ask* and *You Gotta Listen*.

There are so many more stories I'd like to include in this book: Bible stories, personal stories, and many others I've heard since beginning to write this book. Some are downright amazing; all are unique, breathtaking, and encouraging. I am rich in material, but this is not the point. And, it's possible I've belabored the point.

If you're still reading, you get the point: God is speaking to and through all kinds of people. And now you know at least 10 indicators to watch for to know that He is speaking to you or someone near you. Like Jacob, we eventually realize, "Surely the LORD is in this place, and I did not know it." (Genesis 28:16)

If He's speaking, doesn't He intend to be heard?

If He intends to be heard, He can be. He's God.

Isn't it better to find out earlier than later?

It's your turn. Write the rest of the book.

ACKNOWLEDGMENTS

We are full of gratitude to you all because in various ways you made this book possible.

You Gotta Ask Board: These Kingdom-minded and gifted people humbly give wisdom, guidance, encouragement, and ground-game service. They make us possible. Todd Kraft (Chairman), Kyle Woods (Vice Chairman), Emmanuel Navarro (Secretary), Sharolyn Carlson (Treasurer), Lee Lenhardt (Director), John Meyer (Director), Tim Winkle (Director) and Bart Hadder (Consultant, Board Development).

Our Groups and Ministry Partners: We practice the things in this book with these dear people weekly. There are too many to name individually.

Aloha Publishing: Maryanna Young and Heather Goetter (in particular) who are Kingdom-first people and wise guides. And to the whole Aloha team who are diligent and excellent in their craft.

Harold Thomas Foundation: Along with the seed investment to develop this project, they encourage our souls beyond what we deserve.

ABOUT THE AUTHORS

ABOUT PAM

Pam, the Women's Director of You Gotta Ask, Inc., serves in a mentoring role with women throughout the Treasure Valley. She co-founded LIFT, which exists to create impactful, relational events and gatherings that welcome all women and encourage them to live inspired, fearless, and thriving lives. Pam loves creating safe places for women to openly explore tough questions and life challenges. Her favorite hobby is "soul sloshing"—talking with women over a cup of coffee about matters of the heart. She considers it a privilege to walk alongside women to help them discover and embrace who they are and their unique purposes.

ABOUT JON

Jon is the Executive Director for You Gotta Ask, Inc. Jon has partnered in generating "mission startups" including a Christian campus ministry (with CRU and Orem Evangelical Free Church) at BYU in Provo, Utah; a church plant (Riverside Community Church) in Meridian, Idaho; Search Ministries (national), and YOU GOTTA ASK, in Boise. The theme has always been relational evangelism, discipleship, and relational apologetics. Along the way, he earned a Master of Divinity from Western Seminary. Jon loves to train people's hearts and minds, exploring questions about God, life, and manhood. He pioneered the Adventure Dinner, which combines great food shared by interesting people exploring compelling ideas. Jon refuels in the foothills or along the river, hiking, running, walking, and mountain-biking with routine forays into hot yoga. He loves marking up books to glean ideas but does his best thinking on the move. He enjoys great stories and learning from the life experiences of other people.

JON AND PAM AND YOU GOTTA ASK, INC.

Jon and Pam are the authors of *Spiritual Seeds: How to Cultivate Spiritual Wealth Within Your Future Children* (Elevate Publishing, 2015). This book was dedicated to their four adult sons and daughters-in-law. Though empty nesters, they enjoy five grandsons. Both Jon and Pam were raised in agricultural settings: Pam a Nebraska farm girl and Jon the son of a Montana cattleman and horse-racer. They now grow and train people instead of crops and animals. Together, they co-founded You Gotta Ask, Inc. in 2020, inviting men and women to take a next step toward God, starting with compelling questions. In this endeavor they've authored three more supporting books: *You Gotta Ask: How to Have Meaningful Conversations With Anyone Using Compelling Questions* (2021), *You Gotta Ask: The Leader's Guide* (2021), and *The Adventure Dinner Guide: Relationships Matter, People Matter, Truth Matters, Food Matters* (2021).

APPENDIX

Jon's Keys to 10-S Indicators of Hearing God's Voice in the Stories

CHAPTER 1

Samuel's Story in 1 Samuel 3:1-18

It's likely God speaking when it is . . .

1.	Scriptural	1 Samuel 1-2: Building on what God said already
2.	Smarter than you	Way over the head of a young boy's first prophet word
3.	Surprising ("What?")	1 Samuel 3:7: God called Samuel three times, who didn't yet know God
4.	Specific (answer to an ask)	1 Samuel 3:9-10: "Speak, Lord, for your servant is listening
5.	Succinct (one-liner)	1 Samuel 3:11: "Behold, I am going to do a thing in Israel . . ."
6.	Spot-on (customized)	1 Samuel 3:12-18: Eli knew God's judgment was coming
7.	Spiritually fruitful	1 Samuel 3:19: Samuel hearing God as prophet, priest, judge
8.	Supported by spiritually gifted people	Eli, the priest-mentor
9.	Salvation-minded	Samuel's role will deliver Israel
10.	Serving others' best interests	Samuel's calling; judgment on disobedient Eli

Jon's Story of the Joe Gibbs Event

It's likely God speaking when it is . . .

1.	Scriptural	Direct answer to fervent prayer (Matthew 7:7-11)
2.	Smarter than you	I never could have come up with this
3.	Surprising ("What?")	Coach Harsin, then Robin's message, same floor space
4.	Specific (answer to an ask)	Praying, laboring for 18 months
5.	Succinct (one-liner)	"Choose any path . . . because I will be with you; I trust you."
6.	Spot-on (customized)	Exact right time, what I needed—immediately clear
7.	Spiritually fruitful	Great stories: Seeking Kyle Woods, now on YGA board
8.	Supported by spiritually gifted people	Flowed from Robin's spiritual gift
9.	Salvation-minded	Jon delivered from anxiety bondage; many met Jesus
10.	Serving others' best interests	God, via Joe Gibbs and table hosts, touched lives of hundreds

CHAPTER 2

Emmaus Road Story in Luke 24
It's likely God speaking when it is . . .

1.	Scriptural	Luke 24:6-7, 24:25-27, 24:32b, 24:44-46 fulfilled **Matthew 25:31-45**
2.	Smarter than you	Fearful/**foolish**/dense disciples are enlightened
3.	Surprising ("What?")	Luke 24:5: **Terrified**; startled/frightened,
4.	Specific (answer to an ask)	Luke 24:2-3: "They did not find the body . . . perplexed"
5.	Succinct (one-liner)	Luke 24:6: "He is not here, but He has risen."
6.	Spot-on (customized)	Luke 24:32: Hearts burning while He was speaking **to us**
7.	Spiritually fruitful	Luke 24:45-53: "He opened their minds to understand"
8.	Supported by spiritually gifted people	Ephesians **4:7-12**: "Christ ascended . . . gave gifts to men"
9.	Salvation-minded	Luke 24:46-53: "Christ . . . rise . . . forgiveness . . . proclaimed"
10.	Serving others' best interests	Luke 24:47, 24:52: "Forgiveness proclaimed to nations; **joy** . . ."

Gifting the Suburban to Henry
It's likely God speaking when it is . . .

1.	Scriptural	Matthew **25:31-45**: "Done to least of these . . . Jesus"
2.	Smarter than you	God knew **Henry** needed wheels and grace
3.	Surprising ("What?")	"*What?*" I **asked**; surprising, disruptive
4.	Specific (answer to an ask)	"What **should** I do with Suburban? Sell . . . give?" **Perplexed**
5.	Succinct (one-liner)	"Give the Suburban to Henry."
6.	Spot-on (customized)	Henry **can drive** to work for livelihood; he repairs **cars**
7.	Spiritually fruitful	Hard **Henry** touched by grace; enabled to work
8.	Supported by spiritually gifted people	Pastor **Joe and** Chris affirmed vehicle gift to Henry
9.	Salvation-minded	"**Greatest lesson** of God's grace I've **experienced**"
10.	Serving others' best interests	Henry's **livelihood**; elderly ladies' car repairs

CHAPTER 3

Samaritan Woman Story in John 4
It's likely God speaking when it is . . .

1.	Scriptural	Jeremiah 2:13; Daniel 7:13-14, 9:24-25; John 2:24-25
2.	Smarter than you	John 4:15-19, 4: 25-26, 4: 29: "He told me all things . . ."
3.	Surprising ("What?")	John 4:9, 4:19, 4:29, 4:39: Who Jesus is; what He knows
4.	Specific (answer to an ask)	John 4:9, 4:11: Two questions
5.	Succinct (one-liner)	John 4:26: "I who speak to you am He (Messiah)"
6.	Spot-on (customized)	John 4:16-19: "He told me all things I have done."
7.	Spiritually fruitful	John 4:32-42: "Harvest . . . Samaritans believed in Him"
8.	Supported by spiritually gifted people	John 4:36-38: "He who sows . . . reaps . . . rejoice together"
9.	Salvation-minded	John 4:39-42: "More believed because of His word."
10.	Serving others' best interests	John 4:7-10, 4:32-34, 4:42: "Labored" three times in verse 39

Jon's Story at Wild Courage Retreat
It's likely God speaking when it is . . .

1.	Scriptural	Hebrews 4:12-13; Revelation 1:16, 2:12, 2:16, 19:11-16, 21
2.	Smarter than you	Three cowboys hear my story; pre-purchased gifts
3.	Surprising ("What?")	Sword and axe handle gifts; Jesus image in closet
4.	Specific (answer to an ask)	"Holy Spirit, give me a vision of Jesus." (sword-mouth)
5.	Succinct (one-liner)	"Sword . . . cutting . . . power cord on . . . destructive words."
6.	Spot-on (customized)	Pre-prompt to share story; with three cowboys; two gifts
7.	Spiritually fruitful	"Tooled-up . . . special ops . . . freedom fighter for men"
8.	Supported by spiritually gifted people	Britten, specifically; Wild Courage team, generally
9.	Salvation-minded	The man returned to recover the boy-orphan
10.	Serving others' best interests	"Helper" was helped and served; freedom fighter

CHAPTER 4

Bible Story of Jesus Training the Twelve
It's likely God speaking when it is . . .

1.	Scriptural	Mark 13:13: Promise by Jesus: Living Word will give words
2.	Smarter than you	John 14:26: "Helper . . . Holy Spirit will teach you all things"
3.	Surprising ("What?")	Mark 1:22, 7:37: People always "astonished" at His words
4.	Specific (answer to an ask)	John 14:12-14, 15:7-11: "Ask . . . bear fruit . . . My joy in you"
5.	Succinct (one-liner)	Matthew 10:7: "Say, 'The Kingdom of Heaven is at hand.'"
6.	Spot-on (customized)	Mark 13:11: " . . . is not you who speaks but . . . Holy Spirit"
7.	Spiritually fruitful	John 15:16: "I chose . . . appointed you to bear fruit"
8.	Supported by spiritually gifted people	Matthew 9:35, 10:1-7; John 17: "You sent Me . . . I send them."(v.18)
9.	Salvation-minded	Luke 19:9-10: "Son of Man come to seek and save . . . lost."
10.	Serving others' best interests	John 10:16: "I have other sheep . . . they will hear My voice"

Jon's Story at Applebee's
It's likely God speaking when it is . . .

1.	Scriptural	Mark 13:13: "Say whatever is given you . . ."
2.	Smarter than you	Never thought to ask this question; use it a lot now
3.	Surprising ("What?")	Almost immediate answer. "That's a great question!"
4.	Specific (answer to an ask)	"Lord, what do I do with this man?"
5.	Succinct (one-liner)	"Ask him if he's ever had an experience with Me."
6.	Spot-on (customized)	Immediately slumped in chair. Answer: yes!
7.	Spiritually fruitful	Completely changed the conversation, opening it up
8.	Supported by spiritually gifted people	Encouraging employee set meeting for the evangelist
9.	Salvation-minded	God knew what needed to be confronted
10.	Serving others' best interests	*Very* awkward conversation at first—hang in there

CHAPTER 5

Ananias and Saul/Paul Bible Story: Acts 9:1-31
It's likely God speaking when it is . . .

1.	Scriptural	Matthew 10:16-23; Acts 7:58-60, 8:1-3
2.	Smarter than you	Acts 9:1-9, 15-16: "he is a chosen instrument of Mine"
3.	Surprising ("What?")	Acts 9:11: "Arise and go to . . . Saul"
4.	Specific (answer to an ask)	Acts 9:13-14: Implied question about Saul, the persecutor
5.	Succinct (one-liner)	Acts 9:11-15: "Arise and go to Saul . . . chosen instrument"
6.	Spot-on (customized)	Acts 9:4-5, 9:10-19: Exactly what to do and why
7.	Spiritually fruitful	Acts 9:15: "He . . . will bear My name: Gentiles, kings, Israel"
8.	Supported by spiritually gifted people	Acts 6:5-12, 7 (Stephen), 9:10-19 (Ananias)
9.	Salvation-minded	Acts 9:11-31: Saul's conversion and Jesus's proclamation
10.	Serving others' best interests	Acts 7:59-60: Stephen forgiving his murderers; Acts 9:17

Eric and Chris Story at Crossfit
It's likely God speaking when it is . . .

1.	Scriptural	Acts 9:10-11: God tells us to invite/minister to the unlikely
2.	Smarter than you	God speaking to Eric; second prompt very strong
3.	Surprising ("What?")	"Invite Haps to the men's group." Skeptic
4.	Specific (answer to an ask)	Eric praying for Crossfit men and who to invite
5.	Succinct (one-liner)	"Invite Haps to the men's group," twice
6.	Spot-on (customized)	Chris just became aware of men's group; was curious
7.	Spiritually fruitful	Came once, didn't stop; shared with his family
8.	Supported by spiritually gifted people	All the other Crossfit men; others in the men's group
9.	Salvation-minded	God knew Chris was ready; strong prompt twice
10.	Serving others' best interests	Eric took risk with Chris; Chris with Remy; Remy with JP

CHAPTER 6

Bible Story: Matthew 9:35-10:2
It's likely God speaking when it is . . .

1.	Scriptural	Jesus is the Living Word: pray and do as Jesus did
2.	Smarter than you	Matthew 9:37: Jesus knows "the harvest is plentiful"
3.	Surprising ("What?")	Matthew 10:1-2: The twelve are the immediate answer to prayer
4.	Specific (answer to an ask)	Matthew 9:37-38: "Workers are few; beseech the Lord"
5.	Succinct (one-liner)	"Go, preach, saying, 'The Kingdom of heaven is at hand.'"
6.	Spot-on (customized)	"These twelve Jesus sent out after instructing them . . ."
7.	Spiritually fruitful	Acts 17:6: "These men . . . have upset the world . . . here also"
8.	Supported by spiritually gifted people	Ephesians 4:8, 4:11-12
9.	Salvation-minded	Matthew 10:6-8: "Go to the lost sheep . . . preach . . . heal . . . give"
10.	Serving others' best interests	Matthew 9:35-36: "Proclaiming . . . gospel . . . healing . . . compassion"

Tony Ball Prayer Bookmarker Story
It's likely God speaking when it is . . .

1.	Scriptural	Matthew 9:35-38; Romans 10:1; Colossians 4:2-4
2.	Smarter than you	God gave three names to write on bookmarker
3.	Surprising ("What?")	Surprised later when he found the lost bookmarker
4.	Specific (answer to an ask)	Bookmarker invited writing names to pray for
5.	Succinct (one-liner)	Three names came to mind that day
6.	Spot-on (customized)	Years pass; Tony prompted to invite each
7.	Spiritually fruitful	All three came to faith in one summer
8.	Supported by spiritually gifted people	Griz: men's retreat; Dad: Luis Palau; Doug: questions with Jon
9.	Salvation-minded	Prayed for their salvation; then invited the to something
10.	Serving others' best interests	Griz died; Doug was baptized and came to the church; Dad came to the church

CHAPTER 7

Bible Truths: Psalm 23:1-6; Genesis 28:16; John 10:16
It's likely God speaking when it is . . .

1.	Scriptural	Psalm 23; John 10:16; Genesis 28:16; Revelations 3:20
2.	Smarter than you	Psalm 23:1: "The Lord is my Shepherd . . ."
3.	Surprising ("What?")	Psalm 23:5: "He prepares a table before me in the presence of enemies"
4.	Specific (answer to an ask)	"I stand at the door and knock . . . if anyone hears My voice . . ."
5.	Succinct (one-liner)	Genesis 28:16: "Surely, the Lord is in this place, and I did not know it."
6.	Spot-on (customized)	John 10:27: "My sheep hear my voice and I know them . . ."
7.	Spiritually fruitful	John 10:28: "I give eternal life to them . . . shall never perish . . ."
8.	Supported by spiritually gifted people	1 Peter 5:1-2: "Shepherd the flock of God among you . . ."
9.	Salvation-minded	John 10:16: "I have other sheep . . . I must bring them also . . ."
10.	Serving others' best interests	The Shepherd provides, guides, and is with us

Keith the Navy SEAL Medic Story: You Can't Quit!
It's likely God speaking when it is . . .

1.	Scriptural	Genesis 28:16: "The Lord is in this place . . . I did not know it."
2.	Smarter than you	Keith heard exact same wording in two crises moments
3.	Surprising ("What?")	Not expected from a SEAL trainer, or in the dark night, van
4.	Specific (answer to an ask)	Dark night callout
5.	Succinct (one-liner)	"You can't quit!"
6.	Spot-on (customized)	Timing of the voice knew exactly where he was, twice
7.	Spiritually fruitful	Saved his life to save other's lives; still discovering
8.	Supported by spiritually gifted people	Courses to transition to civilian; Steve, Kyle, Jon, etc.
9.	Salvation-minded	Saved his career calling and later his life
10.	Serving others' best interests	19 years, eight tours of duty saving lives as SEAL medic; more

CHAPTER 8

Bible Story: 1 Corinthians 2:9-16; 1 Kings 19
It's likely God speaking when it is . . .

1.	Scriptural	1 Corinthians 2:9, 16; Isaiah 40:13, 64:4, 65:17
2.	Smarter than you	1 Corinthians 1:29-30: "No man boasts . . . by His doing you're in Christ"
3.	Surprising ("What?")	1 Corinthians 2:2: "I know nothing . . . except Jesus Christ . . . crucified"
4.	Specific (answer to an ask)	Acts 18:9-10; 1 Corinthians 2:1-5: Corinthian conversion story
5.	Succinct (one-liner)	1 Corinthians 2:16; Isaiah 40:13: "But we have the mind of Christ."
6.	Spot-on (customized)	1 Corinthians 1:27: "God chose the foolish to shame the wise."
7.	Spiritually fruitful	1 Corinthians 3:6b, 3:7b: "God causes the growth . . ."
8.	Supported by spiritually gifted people	1 Corinthians 3:6: "I planted, Apollos watered . . . God . . . causing growth"
9.	Salvation-minded	1 Corinthians 1:30: "By His doing you are in Christ Jesus"
10.	Serving others' best interests	1 Corinthians 2:1-5: "I know nothing among you except Jesus . . ."

Jon and False Identity Story at the Idaho Capitol
It's likely God speaking when it is . . .

1.	Scriptural	1 Corinthians 2:10-13 (mixing spiritual thoughts/words); Psalm 15:1-2
2.	Smarter than you	30 false identities on yellow pad in one hour
3.	Surprising ("What?")	Jolting timing of good-natured jab, "You can't park there!"
4.	Specific (answer to an ask)	What do I need to know about my true identity?
5.	Succinct (one-liner)	"You can't park there!"
6.	Spot-on (customized)	God using humor via Kyle and Jamie Winship to disrupt me
7.	Spiritually fruitful	Psalm 15:1-2: Living true in God is speaking truth in my heart
8.	Supported by spiritually gifted people	Jamie Winship, IdentityExchange.com; *Fearless Living*
9.	Salvation-minded	Isaiah 43:1-2: Created, formed, named, redeemed, summoned
10.	Serving others' best interests	Living true in God's identity is freedom and fruit-bearing

CHAPTER 9

Bible Story: Elijah Hearing God's Gentle Whisper at Mt. Sinai
It's likely God speaking when it is . . .

1.	Scriptural	1 Kings 19; 1 Corinthians 2:13; Exodus 33-34 (Moses at Mt. Sinai)
2.	Smarter than you	1 Kings 19:8-13: God sent him to Mt. Sinai, asking a question twice
3.	Surprising ("What?")	1 Kings 19:11-12: God's gentle whisper, not earth/wind/fire
4.	Specific (answer to an ask)	1 Kings 19:4, 19:10: He asked God to take his life he is so depressed
5.	Succinct (one-liner)	1 Kings 19:9b, 19:13b: "What are you doing here Elijah?" twice
6.	Spot-on (customized)	Like Moses, Elijah hears God's whisper and two questions
7.	Spiritually fruitful	1 Kings 19:9-14: God confronts "I'm alone" lie; recommissions him
8.	Supported by spiritually gifted people	This story made the canon of Old Testament Scripture
9.	Salvation-minded	1 Kings 19:15-18: His life and ministry saved to anoint kings & Elisha
10.	Serving others' best interests	1 Kings 19:19-21: Mentored Elisha who was twice Elijah in miracles

Pam's Story, God Naming Her Love Activist
It's likely God speaking when it is . . .

1.	Scriptural	Isaiah 43:1, 62:2: "You will be called by a new name"
2.	Smarter than you	"Totally made sense why He would have me do this."
3.	Surprising ("What?")	"Tell me you love me." What? Did I hear you right, God?
4.	Specific (answer to an ask)	Sitting with God. "What do you want me to know . . . do"?
5.	Succinct (one-liner)	"Tell me you love me," and, "Your name is Love Activist."
6.	Spot-on (customized)	"I grew up never saying, 'I love you.'"
7.	Spiritually fruitful	"Something shifted . . . when I told God I loved Him."
8.	Supported by spiritually gifted people	Jon understood Pam's message from God immediately
9.	Salvation-minded	"My . . . joys . . . others discover how much God loves them."
10.	Serving others' best interests	He revealed to me that my name is Love Activist

CHAPTER 10

Bible Passages on Naming and Key Observations
It's likely God speaking when it is . . .

1.	Scriptural	John 10:3: "Sheep hear his voice . . . calls His own . . . by name"
2.	Smarter than you	Psalm 139: Creator God formed all our parts in the womb
3.	Surprising ("What?")	Everyone is joyfully surprised and affirmed, eventually.
4.	Specific (answer to an ask)	Matthew 7:7-11: Ask, seek, knock . . . He gives good gifts
5.	Succinct (one-liner)	Isaiah 43:1: "I have called you by name, you are mine . . ."
6.	Spot-on (customized)	People know it immediately and/or grow into it.
7.	Spiritually fruitful	Deeply connects us to God, clarifying identity and purpose.
8.	Supported by spiritually gifted people	When they hear our name, those around us comprehend it.
9.	Salvation-minded	We are rescued from false self and pseudo-identities.
10.	Serving others' best interests	Being the true me is the best gift I can give others.

Jon Story, God Named "Helper"
It's likely God speaking when it is . . .

1.	Scriptural	Psalm 121:1-2; John 14, 16
2.	Smarter than you	Years prior: Enneagram 2, but underwhelmed by "Helper"
3.	Surprising ("What?")	"Helper." What? Wait, did I come up with it? No! C'mon.
4.	Specific (answer to an ask)	"God, what do you call me?"
5.	Succinct (one-liner)	"Helper." "You realize it's what I call Myself in the Bible, right?"
6.	Spot-on (customized)	Best memories of being with my dad, helping with his work
7.	Spiritually fruitful	God to Jon: "Let me teach you what it means to be a Helper."
8.	Supported by spiritually gifted people	People affirm that I "help" others take a step toward God
9.	Salvation-minded	Psalm 121; John 14, 16: God is called Helper, deliverer, and rescuer
10.	Serving others' best interests	Jamie Winship: "God will only call you a name He would call Himself."

CHAPTER 11

Bible Passage: Daniel 3: Shadrach, Meshach, and Abednego
It's likely God speaking when it is . . .

1.	Scriptural	Deuteronomy 6:4-5; Exodus 20:1-5: "You shall have no other gods before Me."
2.	Smarter than you	Daniel 3:29: "No other god is able to deliver in this way"
3.	Surprising ("What?")	Nonverbal, God present with them in the fiery furnace
4.	Specific (answer to an ask)	Daniel 3:16-18: Seen in, "God is able to deliver us, but if not . . ."
5.	Succinct (one-liner)	Exodus 20:3: God spoke, "You shall have no other gods . . ."
6.	Spot-on (customized)	Daniel 3:25: Four men walking in fire without harm
7.	Spiritually fruitful	Daniel 3:28-4:3: Nebuchadnezzar blesses most high God
8.	Supported by spiritually gifted people	Unless we count Daniel writing and the King promoting them
9.	Salvation-minded	Inspired observers of Israel's God (the Most High). He delivers.
10.	Serving others' best interests	Their obedience raised everyone's trust in the Lord

Kent Bader's Story
It's likely God speaking when it is . . .

1.	Scriptural	Mark 13:13: "Say whatever is given you . . ."
2.	Smarter than you	Kent opened his mouth not knowing what would come out
3.	Surprising ("What?")	Kent was surprised, but later listeners were even more so—brilliant
4.	Specific (answer to an ask)	Kent was praying for his witnesses, open doors
5.	Succinct (one-liner)	"If I'm to spend money on a woman . . . will be my wife and girls."
6.	Spot-on (customized)	Unknown in the moment, but disarmed strip club energy
7.	Spiritually fruitful	Respect, trust grew; colleague surprisingly defended Kent
8.	Supported by spiritually gifted people	All who hear the story are empowered, especially Kent's wife
9.	Salvation-minded	Kent put his job on the line to obey God, but God solidified it.
10.	Serving others' best interests	All his listeners, his wife and daughters, all readers

CHAPTER 12

Bible Passage: 1 Peter 3:15: Being Prepared in a Hostile Culture
It's likely God speaking when it is . . .

1.	Scriptural	Acts 1:8: "You shall be My witnesses"; 1 Peter 3: "Always ready . . ."
2.	Smarter than you	If we "set apart Christ as Lord in our hearts"
3.	Surprising ("What?")	1 Peter 3:9, 3:13: We return blessing for insult, suffer for doing good
4.	Specific (answer to an ask)	1 Peter 3:15b: Be prepared to share with others the reason you have hope.
5.	Succinct (one-liner)	Prepared account of our hope and what is most important
6.	Spot-on (customized)	Living in a way that evokes others asking about our hope
7.	Spiritually fruitful	1 Peter 4:8-9: "Fervent in love . . . hospitable . . . stewards of grace"
8.	Supported by spiritually gifted people	1 Peter 3:8, 3:15d: "All of you be harmonious . . . gentle . . . reverent [etc.]"
9.	Salvation-minded	1 Peter 4:6: "The gospel for this purpose has been preached . . ."
10.	Serving others' best interests	1 Peter 4:11: "Whoever speaks . . . serves . . . in all things God glorified"

Scott Greco's Story
It's likely God speaking when it is . . .

1.	Scriptural	Acts 1:8: "You shall be My witnesses . . ."; 1 Peter 3: "Always ready . . ."
2.	Smarter than you	God gave words ahead; Scott didn't know for who or when
3.	Surprising ("What?")	Mostly to us who hear the story, but also the aggressor
4.	Specific (answer to an ask)	Scott had been praying for his witness before SCOTUS case
5.	Succinct (one-liner)	"What's most important thing in your life? . . . Mine is Jesus."
6.	Spot-on (customized)	Perfectly disarmed aggressor, respectful and according to Jesus
7.	Spiritually fruitful	It left a door open with the man; model of witness at work
8.	Supported by spiritually gifted people	Made his colleague smile and listeners see its brilliance
9.	Salvation-minded	Stood with Jesus as most important; left the man thinking
10.	Serving others' best interests	Credible Jesus-witness; integrity in work authority

CHAPTER 13

Bible Passages: Isaiah 61:1-2 (quoted in Luke 4:18-19): Inauguration of Jesus's Public Ministry

It's likely God speaking when it is . . .

1.	Scriptural	Among 61 major prophecies, Jesus fulfills Isaiah 61 on six fronts
2.	Smarter than you	Isaiah prophecies made 700-plus years before His ministry
3.	Surprising ("What?")	Luke 4:21: "Today this Scripture . . . fulfilled in Your hearing"
4.	Specific (answer to an ask)	The Jewish people had been praying for Messiah's return
5.	Succinct (one-liner)	Today this Scripture . . . [is] fulfilled.
6.	Spot-on (customized)	Luke 4:22-30: Greatly disrupted His hometown synagogue
7.	Spiritually fruitful	Many would come to believe in Him as Messiah eventually
8.	Supported by spiritually gifted people	John the Baptist: John 1:35-37, 11:1-6, quoting Isaiah 35:5f, 61:1
9.	Salvation-minded	Isaiah 61:1-2: plus His name is Yeshua: YHWH is salvation
10.	Serving others' best interests	Jesus came for our salvation

Jon Story at Rachel's Vineyard Post-Abortion Healing Retreat

It's likely God speaking when it is . . .

1.	Scriptural	Mark 13:11: "Don't be anxious . . . say whatever is given you."
2.	Smarter than you	God knew Cathleen would whack me on the head.
3.	Surprising ("What?")	Premonition: ready for anything; Role: broken older man
4.	Specific (answer to an ask)	"Father, what do you want me to know for the role play?"
5.	Succinct (one-liner)	"Be ready for anything; take whatever comes to you."
6.	Spot-on (customized)	Surprises all weekend, especially new names written on rocks
7.	Spiritually fruitful	All participants: free, joyful, affirmed, loved on Sunday a.m.
8.	Supported by spiritually gifted people	5-1 ratio: hospitality, counselors, pastors, prayers, pastors
9.	Salvation-minded	Liberation, release, salvation, deliverance
10.	Serving others' best interests	Team fully there for retreatants and them for each other

CHAPTER 14

Bible Passages: Luke 1-2: Birth Announcements of Jesus and John
It's likely God speaking when it is . . .

1.	Scriptural	Malachi 3:1, 4:6 (John); Isaiah 7:14, 9:7; Daniel 7:13-14 (Jesus)
2.	Smarter than you	Jesus and John named, anointed, called, prophesied of before birth
3.	Surprising ("What?")	Luke 1:13, 1:31: Aging Elizabeth and virgin Mary "will bear a son"
4.	Specific (answer to an ask)	Lifelong-barren Elizabeth; Luke 1:38: Mary "bondslave"
5.	Succinct (one-liner)	"Conceive . . . bear a son . . . Jesus . . . Son of God . . . reign forever."
6.	Spot-on (customized)	Scandalous: virgin and aged; Luke 1:42: "Blessed among women . . ."
7.	Spiritually fruitful	Forerunner to God becoming man to save men, Luke 1:32-33
8.	Supported by spiritually gifted people	Angel Gabriel; Zacharias and Elizabeth; Mary and Joseph
9.	Salvation-minded	Luke 1:68-69; 1:46-49
10.	Serving others' best interests	Son of God, Savior-Redeemer, and Eternal King of mankind

Jon's Dad Story, Hearing Voices in Spiritual Conflict

This isn't a "hearing God" story by which we can use the 10-S indicators. It does raise awareness about dark side voices. My dad's testimony of coming to Christ, told in our first book, *Spiritual Seeds*, is loaded with hearing God indicators, but we chose not to include it here.

CHAPTER 15

Bible Passages

It's likely God speaking when it is . . .

1.	Scriptural	Jeremiah 33:3; Matthew 7:7-11; Zephaniah 3:17
2.	Smarter than you	Matthew 7: Parents know to give good gifts? How much more does God?
3.	Surprising ("What?")	Jeremiah 33: Promise to exile-bound Israel, "I will answer you"
4.	Specific (answer to an ask)	Bold invitations: call to Me; ask, seek, and knock promises
5.	Succinct (one-liner)	Call to me and I will answer you and show you
6.	Spot-on (customized)	Matthew 7:11: "Good gifts" as a good, disciplining parent (Jeremiah 33)
7.	Spiritually fruitful	Matthew 7:7: Given to you, found, opened to you; Matthew 7:12: Golden rule
8.	Supported by spiritually gifted people	Matthew 7:9-11: Parents; Zephaniah 3:17b: "Quiet in His love"
9.	Salvation-minded	Zephaniah 3: God is loving, victorious, exultant warrior with you
10.	Serving others' best interests	Jeremiah 33:3b: I will answer you and show you . . .

Karen's Story Hearing God in the Shower

It's likely God speaking when it is . . .

1.	Scriptural	Jeremiah 33:3; Matthew 7:7-11; Zephaniah 3:17
2.	Smarter than you	Bible verses, cross—it was there, *but I just didn't get it.*
3.	Surprising ("What?")	1) In the shower? 2) God loves my kids more than I do.
4.	Specific (answer to an ask)	Asking and seeking God for weeks; reading; searching
5.	Succinct (one-liner)	"I was there for you the whole time . . . loved you through all." "I love you, My daughter . . . My children too . . . so much."
6.	Spot-on (customized)	So self-reliant—God spoke specifically to Karen's heart pain
7.	Spiritually fruitful	Liberation, joy, baptism, serving Debra at women's event
8.	Supported by spiritually gifted people	Pam, Cindy, and Dee
9.	Salvation-minded	Karen's salvation and her burden for her family and others
10.	Serving others' best interests	Served her liberation and to be a fighter for others too

CHAPTER 16

Bible Passages

It's likely God speaking when it is . . .

1.	Scriptural	Genesis 28:12-16 fulfills Genesis 12:1-3, 15:5-6, 17:1-8, 8:18, 22:17-18
2.	Smarter than you	Genesis 32:29-30: God to Jacob, "Why . . . ask My name?" You know
3.	Surprising ("What?")	Genesis 28:16: "Surely the Lord is in this place . . . I did not know it."
4.	Specific (answer to an ask)	Genesis 32:11, 32:26: "Deliver me . . . will not let you go unless . . . bless me."
5.	Succinct (one-liner)	Genesis 32:28a: "Name no longer Jacob, but Israel . . . striven . . . prevailed"
6.	Spot-on (customized)	Genesis 32:28b: named Israel: striven/wrestled with God and prevailed
7.	Spiritually fruitful	Genesis 32:9-12; Numbers 6:24-26: Jacob models blessing his sons
8.	Supported by spiritually gifted people	Genesis 33:5b, 33:11: God dealt graciously with me; Genesis 32:10: Unworthy
9.	Salvation-minded	Genesis 32:9-11, 32:30: I've seen God face to face, yet my life is preserved
10.	Serving others' best interests	Genesis 48:8-49, 1-33: "Jacob blessed . . . everyone . . . appropriate to him."

Jason's Gift Story

It's likely God speaking when it is . . .

1.	Scriptural	Numbers 6:24-26; Luke 15:20, 15:22; Malachi 4:6
2.	Smarter than you	I had no idea what to do. I was desperate.
3.	Surprising ("What?")	"Get him a gift"; exactly what and where to buy
4.	Specific (answer to an ask)	Almost immediate
5.	Succinct (one-liner)	Buy the King's baseball glove gumball machine
6.	Spot-on (customized)	Jason's love language of gifts was known to me
7.	Spiritually fruitful	Found out the result years later
8.	Supported by spiritually gifted people	Pam's Moms in Prayer weekly prayers
9.	Salvation-minded	Foundational to salvation; broke our separation
10.	Serving others' best interests	It served him then; me, forever

CHAPTER 17

Bible Passages: Isaiah 43:1, 62:2; Acts 13:9
It's likely God speaking when it is . . .

1.	Scriptural	Isaiah 43:1: "Thus says the Lord . . ."; Isaiah 62:2: "New name Lord designates"
2.	Smarter than you	Isaiah 43:1a: "Your Creator, Jacob . . . He who formed you, Israel"
3.	Surprising ("What?")	Isaiah 43:1c: "I have called you by name; you are Mine!"
4.	Specific (answer to an ask)	Isaiah 32:11, 32:26: "Deliver me . . . will not let you go unless . . . bless me."
5.	Succinct (one-liner)	Isaiah 43:1: "I have redeemed you . . . called . . . by name . . . you're Mine!"
6.	Spot-on (customized)	Isaiah 43:4: "You are precious in My sight . . . honored . . . I love you"
7.	Spiritually fruitful	Isaiah 43:1b, 5a: "Do not fear, for I am with you"
8.	Supported by spiritually gifted people	E.g., Saul to Paul, Acts 13:1-13: Antioch Church and Barnabus
9.	Salvation-minded	Isaiah 43:1b: "I have redeemed you," Isaiah 43:3,11: "your Savior"
10.	Serving others' best interests	Isaiah 43:10: "You are My witnesses . . . servants . . . chosen"

Sieloff Family's Name Story
It's likely God speaking when it is . . .

1.	Scriptural	Isaiah 43:1, 62:2
2.	Smarter than you	We wouldn't have come up with these names for ourselves
3.	Surprising ("What?")	Ashlyn started smiling. "I think I just heard my name."
4.	Specific (answer to an ask)	Each asked, "Father, what do you call me?"
5.	Succinct (one-liner)	God's clear answer for each person
6.	Spot-on (customized)	With each person, we all say, "Of course!"
7.	Spiritually fruitful	Ashlyn is lit up, jumping into designing, and has a mentor
8.	Supported by spiritually gifted people	Her parents; Jamie Winship (book); Jon and Pam
9.	Salvation-minded	From uncertainty in purpose to affirmed in God's design
10.	Serving others' best interests	Prestyn and Chris guiding high school seniors hearing names

CHAPTER 18

Bible Passages: 1 Kings 3; Proverbs 16:9, 19:21; 1 Corinthians 2:13b, 16b

It's likely God speaking when it is . . .

1.	Scriptural	Deuteronomy 17:18-20 is God's warning to Kings through Moses
2.	Smarter than you	1 Kings 3:5: Lord appeared to Solomon in a night dream
3.	Surprising ("What?")	1 Kings 3:5: "Ask what you wish me to give you."
4.	Specific (answer to an ask)	1 Kings 3:9: "Give your servant a hearing heart to judge your people."
5.	Succinct (one-liner)	1 Kings 3:10-12: "Because you asked this thing . . . be it done to you."
6.	Spot-on (customized)	1 Kings 3:7: "King in place of David . . . a little child . . . I do not know . . ."
7.	Spiritually fruitful	1 Kings 3:16-4:34: God-given wisdom, world influence, prosperity
8.	Supported by spiritually gifted people	1 Kings 4:1-7, 4:24-25 (King's administration)
9.	Salvation-minded	1 Kings 3:15: Burnt peace offerings before the Lord, and feast
10.	Serving others' best interests	1 Kings 3:16-34: Great wisdom shared: person/print; world impact

Jon's Strategic Plan Anxiety Story

It's likely God speaking when it is . . .

1.	Scriptural	Proverbs 16:9, 19:21; 1 Corinthians 2:10-16
2.	Smarter than you	God's protection in plans, body of Christ listening together
3.	Surprising ("What?")	Name James O. Fraser came to me in my sleep
4.	Specific (answer to an ask)	Why my anxiety about our strategic initiatives?
5.	Succinct (one-liner)	"If this is your ministry, the sooner it dies the better."
6.	Spot-on (customized)	Exactly what I needed to move forward
7.	Spiritually fruitful	Free: God can do more in a snap than missionary in a lifetime
8.	Supported by spiritually gifted people	1 Corinthians 2:13b, 2:16b: We have the mind of Christ
9.	Salvation-minded	Planning together to invite others to take next step to God
10.	Serving others' best interests	Serves the board, me and those we are reaching

CHAPTER 19

Bible Passages: Psalm 19; Romans 1:1-20; Matthew 4:19
It's likely God speaking when it is . . .

1.	Scriptural	Matthew 4:19; Romans 1:1-20
2.	Smarter than you	Voiceless speech: Creation; Gospel words; conscience
3.	Surprising ("What?")	Matthew 4:19: "fishers of men" compelling; they left their nets
4.	Specific (answer to an ask)	Before Matthew 4:19, they asked Jesus, "Where are you staying?"
5.	Succinct (one-liner)	John 1:35: Jesus: "Come and you will see." They stayed the day.
6.	Spot-on (customized)	"I'll make you fishers of men," to fisherman
7.	Spiritually fruitful	Andrew invited Simon Peter to see Messiah for himself
8.	Supported by spiritually gifted people	Ephesians 4:7-8, 4:11: "He gave gifts to men" (His disciples)
9.	Salvation-minded	Matthew 28:18-20: He made disciples to make disciples of nations
10.	Serving others' best interests	Romans 1:14-16: Witnesses are eager, obligated, not ashamed

John Meyer's Listening to God in Creation and Fishing for Men Story
It's likely God speaking when it is . . .

1.	Scriptural	Matthew 4:19: "Follow Me and I'll make you fishers of men"
2.	Smarter than you	"Do you want to exchange this for a life with Me?"
3.	Surprising ("What?")	"I had a dream as a kid I'd live in Idaho." (What is Idaho?)
4.	Specific (answer to an ask)	Fish for men: "Lord, make me bold in Idaho. What do you want me to do more of in Idaho?"
5.	Succinct (one-liner)	Answer: "Start with your grandkids."
6.	Spot-on (customized)	John's grandkids love hunting and fishing with him
7.	Spiritually fruitful	"Things go better with Jesus and those who live in His word"
8.	Supported by spiritually gifted people	John does a variety of mission outreaches, parachurch organizations
9.	Salvation-minded	"Be where there's food and oxygen in your fishing for men"
10.	Serving others' best interests	The message in Israel informed the Cuba experience

Notes

Made in United States
Troutdale, OR
12/10/2023

15646175R00146